God's
daughters

Lucy!
LOVED sharing
a dorm with you
this year... BADGER.
←2Corinthians 12:9
HFytche

Text copyright © Hannah Fytche 2016
The author asserts the moral right to be identified as the author of this work

Published by
The Bible Reading Fellowship
15 The Chambers, Vineyard
Abingdon OX14 3FE
United Kingdom
Tel: +44 (0)1865 319700
Email: enquiries@brf.org.uk
Website: www.brf.org.uk
BRF is a Registered Charity

ISBN 978 0 85746 409 5

First published 2016
10 9 8 7 6 5 4 3 2 1 0
All rights reserved

Acknowledgements
Unless otherwise stated, scripture quotations are taken from The Holy Bible,
New International Version (Anglicised edition) copyright © 1979, 1984, 2011
by Biblica. Used by permission of Hodder & Stoughton Publishers, an Hachette
UK company. All rights reserved. 'NIV' is a registered trademark of Biblica. UK
trademark number 1448790.

Scripture taken from *THE MESSAGE*. Copyright © 1993, 1994, 1995, 1996, 2000,
2001, 2002. Used by permission of NavPress Publishing Group.

Cover photo: lightstock.com

A catalogue record for this book is available from the British Library

Printed and bound by CPI Group (UK) Ltd, Croydon CR0 4YY

God's
daughters
Loved, held, accepted, enough

Hannah Fytche

Contents

Foreword

God's Daughters is a book that is long overdue, in my opinion. For too long I have been mentoring and chatting with young women and men who struggle in relating their faith to their everyday experiences. They know what they should believe about themselves—many have been told often enough—but they find it so hard when the noise of their culture drowns out what God is saying through his word and through the church. It will be great to have this resource to use with the young women I work with, especially as it is the voice of a young woman speaking through the pages of the book.

Hannah has captured some of the most common feelings that young women struggle with, and is able to unpack what God is really saying to them about who they are and what they might be facing in their lives. She does this in a very structured way with the 'big picture' and 'close-up' sessions, bringing the subject of each chapter into focus. The other two elements—'what God says' and 'headphones time'—help young women to ground what is being said in a very practical way.

The subjects covered are issues that young women talk about a lot, so it is great to see them being addressed by someone of their own age. The book comes across as peer-to-peer encouragement rather than someone older telling them how it should be. However, it will be interesting to see what older women get from this book too, as, apart from the chapter on schools, the issues are relevant to us all. Also, although Hannah is writing for young women who are Christians, people of no faith will be equally well able to relate to the subjects covered.

The book is written in a very readable style and intersperses biblical material with the points for reflection. The story of Elijah at the beginning of the book helps to set the scene and encourages us to continue reading.

My passion is to see all young women and girls enter into everything that God has in store for them and to achieve their God-given potential. Sadly, they are often restricted by what they think of themselves—feeling that they are never quite 'good enough'—so how can we help them to throw off these lies and walk in freedom? This book, I believe, will be really helpful in that process.

I want to see young women resting in God's love and knowing themselves to be completely loved and accepted by the Lord of all creation. This knowledge will make them bold and fearless in their service in God's kingdom. Well done, Hannah, for writing a book that is so much needed in contemporary society!

Sharon Prior
Senior Tutor at Moorlands College; co-founder of Sophia Network

Enough!

Dust coated his clothes and skin, enveloping him in a strange, hot stickiness. He was running for his life, sandals slapping against the desert floor and the soles of his feet, carrying him deep into the wilderness. Only recently God had used him to reinstate his name in Israel, first proving the Baal prophets wrong and then giving the order for their deaths. This is why he was running—or walking, now, as he came towards a broom bush. He sat down underneath it, letting the low branches scratch his back and the leaves form a canopy over his head. He lifted a dust-covered and weary face up to the sky, and said, 'Enough, God! I've had enough. I don't want to live any more; take my life.'

Elijah promptly fell asleep under the broom bush, exhausted and craving death. Death would be his escape.

Something soft, light and pure brushed over his skin and he awoke. A voice spoke: it was an angel sent by the God whom he'd begged to kill him.

'Get up and eat.'

He raised himself up on his elbows and looked wearily around. By his head he found some bread and water. He ate and drank, and lay back down.

Some time later, the angel woke him again.

'Get up and eat, for the journey is too much for you.'

Again, Elijah found bread and water, and he ate and drank. This time he felt new energy coursing through his veins, strengthening his worn-out body. He stood up in the wilderness, squinted towards the distant mountain of God, and began to walk.

＊ ■ ＊

This is a story from 1 Kings 19, in the Old Testament, about Elijah the prophet. He was a man who stood up for God radically and bravely, yet here he is worn out and ready to give up, content just to lie on the ground. He has had enough and lets God know about it. How *human*! Do you feel like that sometimes? Like you've had enough of being worn out and chased by the pressures of life, and you just want to lie down and sleep?

I first heard this story at a time when I was struggling with my faith and even with getting dressed in the morning, as I had just had major surgery on my right arm. I sat down with my best friend and told him, 'I just don't want to think about anything any more.' Despite my reluctance to listen, he began to tell me the story of Elijah lying under a broom bush. (I had no idea what a broom bush was at the time, which did confuse me a little. Google it—it helps!)

Later on, I wrote the words 'Get up and eat' in my prayer journal in wobbly left-handed writing. I kept returning to them again and again, to motivate myself to get out of bed every morning and get dressed with only one working arm. They gave me strength to stand up in my wilderness of a broken arm and a struggling faith, squint towards the distant face of God and begin to walk.

But the story doesn't end there.

＊ ■ ＊

The stone of the mountainside cave cooled with the night as Elijah sat looking out at the stars. God spoke.

'What are you doing here, Elijah?'

'I have worked my heart out for you, God, but the Israelites have thrown your promises into the dirt and have piled your altars, torn and broken, there with them. I am the only one left, and now they're trying to kill me!'

'Come out of your cave, Elijah. I am about to pass by.'

Elijah stood outside the cave and was nearly blown back in again as a mighty wind ripped rocks off the mountainside. But God was not in the wind.

Elijah stayed standing where he was, but only just! An earthquake rumbled through the mountain and shook him to the core. But God was not in the earthquake.

Elijah looked out again into the night. When would God pass by? Suddenly, a fire crackled and roared through the night sky, almost singeing Elijah's dusty beard. But God was not in the fire.

And then, a whisper rippled through the air. Elijah pulled his cloak over his face and moved further out of his cave. From the gentle, calm sound, God spoke.

'What are you doing here, Elijah?'

Again, Elijah explained himself, and God gave him instructions to go to Damascus and anoint new people as kings and prophets. Inspired by God's voice and obedient to his power, Elijah began to walk, this time away from the mountain.

Soon after my best friend told me this story, I learnt a new word: 'zephyr'. A zephyr is a slight movement of the air or a gentle breeze passing by, almost like a breath. Elijah felt the breath of God that night and heard his voice speak out of the gentleness. This was unexpected: Elijah was on a mountainside and God was going to pass by. If everything was as we might expect, surely God's voice would be dramatic, loud and striking, much like the wind or the earthquake or the fire?

But God chose a zephyr to speak to Elijah, which was exactly what he needed. Elijah had been running from a warrant for his death and a people who had rejected God, and he was frustrated and tired of life. He didn't need God to instruct him through loud fires, earthquakes or winds; he needed God's gentle love, encouragement and peace.

If you think about it, the earthquake, fire and wind were much like the pressures that Elijah was running from. They were loud, demanding, scary and exhausting, and God wasn't in them. God's voice was the gentle one among them all, the calm breeze that passed by and encouraged Elijah, giving him strength to walk forwards.

Think about your life for a moment. Do you ever collapse on your bed, giving up on the schoolwork that is just too difficult but that you need to get perfect? Do you ever feel under so much pressure to be prettier, cleverer or holier that you feel you just might break? Do you ever feel as if you're not good enough for other people, and they will never love or accept you? Do you feel as if you're the one who has to change, to solve the problems and get it all right?

I definitely feel like that sometimes.

I am writing this book to tell you that you don't have to feel like that any more. God doesn't want us to live craving love and fearing failure, when he already loves us and forgives our mistakes. We can tune out the rushing winds, rumbling earthquakes and roaring fires of life and tune into God. Maybe this can become a way of life, something you and I can both learn to be—tuned into God's gentle, zephyr-like voice, free to rest in his love and grace every single day.

In this book I have taken six issues that most of us encounter as young women in our culture: school, image, friends, family, church and our personal relationship with God. Each of these areas comes with its own pressures, and we can often feel as if our teachers, family, friends or even God expect us to be better than we feel inside. If we don't meet these expectations, we think we need to work harder in order to be loved and accepted. But this is not true.

In each chapter, I write a reminder of who God is and who he says we are, and what he says about the voices around us that demand so much and leave us feeling inadequate and exhausted. In most of the chapters, I do this in four ways:

- Looking at the **big picture**: I discuss what the problem is. How do your school, family or friends put pressure on you to work harder to be 'good enough'? What do these voices say?
- Zooming in to the **close-up**: through real-life stories, I unpick the problem in more detail and show you that you are not alone. We all experience pressure and we are all looking for unconditional love.
- Focusing on **what God says**: this part of the chapter looks at the Bible and opens up what God's voice says about the pressures you are under.
- Giving you **headphones time**: finally, there are some questions you can use to spend time reflecting and listening to God's voice. My youth leader once told me that I need to put headphones on, so that I can block out the busyness and loudness of the world and just focus on hearing God's voice.

This is my prayer for me as I write this book, and you as you read it. May we realise that we have had enough of trying to be good enough. May we let God strengthen us to keep walking. May we listen to God's gentle voice and relearn what it is that makes us free, and may we be encouraged to lift our weary eyes up to God and dwell in his amazing grace.

Loved enough... even at a school desk

Because God has made us for himself, we are restless until we rest in him.

AUGUSTINE OF HIPPO[1]

The big picture

You step through the tall metal gates, your breath warming the cold early morning air in front of you. You pull your coat more closely around you as you are greeted by loud voices calling across courtyards, a riot of conversations waking you up to another busy day. The familiar buildings enclose you, and you pause, breathe in and anticipate the hours ahead of learning and conversing and working hard.

School days begin like this, with an anticipation of what lies ahead. Is it something you look forward to, or something that you dread as you wake up on a weekday morning?

For me, the word 'school' contains a world of emotions and experiences. It's exciting to have the opportunity to study the subjects I love, discovering new ideas and making connections between literature, language, theology and life. (I study English Literature, English Language and Religious Studies.) It's fantastic to be able to learn alongside friends, too, enjoying breaks and lunchtimes, relaxing and messing about amid the hard graft of lessons and study periods.

But with the experience of school comes a certain dread

as well. How much will I be asked to do today? Does my uniform look acceptable, impressive, smart enough? Will I get everything right? It's worse if I'm really tired. I have to drag my exhausted self out of bed just to endure yet another day with teachers and fellow students when I really want to be curled up reading a book... or writing one.

So 'school' is truly a word with mixed connotations, inspiring both reluctance and readiness as I eat my breakfast each morning. Maybe you feel the same? If you're home-schooled, it will be different, of course, but I think we all have an idea of how much time, energy and effort school consumes. It's definitely a privilege, especially when you think about all of the girls around the world who don't have access to education, but sometimes the process of being educated can feel more of a burden than a blessing.

Currently, I am in the process of deciding what to do after school. While some of my friends are taking gap years or finding apprenticeships, I've decided to apply to university. Making 'the university decision' is time-consuming and sometimes stressful, and the thought of leaving home for a big city next year is both terrifying and exciting. As I go to a smallish school in the middle of the countryside, I am definitely looking forward to living somewhere new, with new people and a different lifestyle rhythm to learn. Leaving my school will also be hard, having walked the same corridors for seven years. Only a couple of weeks ago, my friends and I realised that, by the end of this academic year, we will have spent 14 years at school in total, across both primary and secondary school. This is equivalent to 504 weeks, which equals 2520 days, which means that we will have spent about 17,640 hours in school. This seems like a phenomenal amount of time!

It's amazing, as well as slightly odd, to think about how much time we spend with teachers. They have a huge influence on our lives as well as on our exam grades; throughout our teenage years, school plays a huge part in shaping our identities, teaching us social skills and giving us a plethora of experiences that contribute massively to who we become. This can be both a good and a bad thing: although school is a positive place for the most part, it can also be a great source of pressure.

The pressure begins with those first few steps through the school gates, as the noise of many voices reaches your ears, immediately reminding you of school's importance and the attention you must pay it for the next six or seven hours. School is not a quiet place; it is always busy and bustling. I know that I can never find a completely quiet space in which to get work done or just take some peaceful time for myself. Only a couple of days ago, I thought I'd found a nice quiet spot to sit and write, until about 150 Year 12s came and joined me after their assembly had finished early. That definitely made it harder to get work done.

Teachers, classmates and even results papers can become voices too, in the sense that they demand your time, attention and emotional energy. These voices are unavoidable. They're an everyday part of school life and they are important: they give you both praise and criticism to help you develop to the next level of your learning.

Sometimes, however, these voices seem to shout, clamouring for attention and the top spot in your priorities. Surely you have to listen to their every word to know if you're getting everything right or if you're doing well enough? I know from my own experience how much of your 'ear-space' these voices take up, often making you feel you have to try harder, work longer and get consistent grades in order to keep up with the crowd or please your teachers.

I'm feeling this especially now, as it's my last year at school: it has the potential to be the most difficult yet. I need to achieve the grades that universities want, in order to have a future, a life—or at least that's how school presents it.

It seems to me that success has been presented like this throughout my school life. In primary school, the next reading level was of the Utmost Importance, and class projects needed to be Just Perfect. The message has been continually reinforced since then, my school life becoming a game of exam performance and striving to do better and be cleverer. Perhaps you've felt this pressure through sports clubs or academic study or performing arts.

I'm not saying it's bad that school pushes us to our full potential, making sure that we are doing the best we possibly can. It is bad, however, when we feel as if our best is not good enough for school teachers or exam boards, and when we push ourselves to work harder to reach the unattainable goal of 'perfection' and secure our future pathways through life.

For me, there was one teacher who particularly emphasised the importance and pressure of getting things exactly right all the time. This teacher taught me for GCSE and was famous for her excellent, successful teaching and the results her students gained, but also notorious for her strict style. You had to pay constant attention in case she picked on you for an answer, and if you didn't know it, you'd be humiliated in front of the whole class. You have a teacher like that, right?

This teacher wrote all of the notes on the board for us to copy into our books, meaning that there were long periods of time when her back was to us. One such time, a troublesome boy decided to play catch with his pen instead of using it to write down the notes. It didn't bother us; we were used to it. But then, he dropped his pen. At the sound of it hitting the floor, our teacher turned around and glared at the boy ominously. She looked about ready to explode.

'Stop throwing the pen! Write your notes! Because if you don't get these notes, you won't learn the information, and if you don't learn the information, you will lose marks in your exam. And if that happens, you might not get the grade you need to do A Levels or go to university. And if you can't do that... you'll never get anywhere in life!'

Well, that escalated quickly. He'd only dropped a pen!

Because of its dramatic nature, our teacher's rant had the desired effect: the boy stopped throwing the pen and we were all silent and extremely attentive for the rest of the lesson. An important thing was highlighted to us by the teacher that day: every single moment we spend in school is important, and if we don't pay attention for every single second, we will fail.

Although this is not actually the case—you can play catch with a pen and still learn lessons—the teacher brought to the surface the way most of us are made to feel about school and exams. Those 17,640 hours we spend in classrooms become our life, and everything—our worth, our success, our acceptance—rides on our exam results. We are made to feel that without top grades, we won't reach the top jobs or be successful enough in life. In short, anything less than an A* is just not good enough.

Is this familiar to you? This feeling of constant pressure to do better in school in order to be seen as 'good enough'?

The sweaty hands and thudding heart as we enter exam halls are familiar to us. They show our fear of not doing well and of not getting the grades we need to climb to a higher level at school. This isn't a healthy way to live, constantly striving for teachers' praise or higher grades. Praise is good, of course, and it is great to want to do well and reach your full potential. However, things get stressful and pressurised when praise, grades and, ultimately, acceptance become the biggest goal of your life. It's when you feel as if you're not good enough without that target grade that things begin to get bad.

The close-up

Being in school and talking to people has opened my eyes to the fact that *it isn't just me* who struggles with the standards that schools set. I've included some stories here about school pressures and their effects. As you read, ask yourself this: where is the pressure coming from in each story?

———— ▦ ■ ▦ ————

Year 11 has begun for Katie and, so far, it's the most important school year she's encountered. It's really tough. She's taking Business Studies, Art and Graphics, as well as the 'core subjects' of Maths, Sciences and English. Art and Graphics in particular bring with them a ton of work; each week Katie receives huge projects to complete and hand in to be graded. Every evening she spends hours on homework, going to sleep late and waking up tired, yet she is still expected to have perfect concentration in her lessons the next day.

Recently, she has been set an English assignment in which she has to make a presentation to her class. Katie never feels confident speaking to large groups of people; now, even weeks before the presentation is due, the nerves are already kicking in. Her thoughts repeat: 'What if I stumble on my words or make mistakes? I'll embarrass myself in front of all of them! I won't be good enough.'

She's feeling the pressure of having to perform brilliantly all the time, and it's just a bit too much.

———————— ▫ ▪ ▫ ————————

The students of 12J amble into the room and take their seats, chattering about what they did in the last lesson a week ago. As they get out paper and pens, ready to take notes, their teacher enters. Silence descends. Suddenly, they are only a bunch of 16- and 17-year-olds under the power and scrutiny of a new teacher they've seen only twice before. Taking his position behind his desk, their teacher looks expectantly around the room.

'So, can anyone remind me what we did last lesson?' A querying look passes across his face, as if he is trying to remember as well (although it's obvious he knows already). He waits for someone to answer, yet receives only silence. The students avoid all eye contact and leave their hands down; no one wants to say a word.

They all know what they did: only minutes before, they were discussing it among themselves. However, they are reluctant to share, *just in case they get it wrong*. If they answer incorrectly, surely their teacher will judge them. Doom and disaster will begin their approach in the form of Seriously Major Embarrassment.

The lesson continues awkwardly, silently. Everyone breathes a great sigh of relief as they exit the anxious atmosphere at the end of the morning, happy that they no longer have to answer questions correctly.

Fast-forward a few days, and you see the same class enter the same room, chattering about the awkwardness of the previous occasion. This time, as the teacher enters, silence descends again but is soon replaced by nervous giggles bubbling from the lips of 12J. Their teacher has his tie on backwards! Is it an epic wardrobe fail or a lack of organisation? Can the guy not even dress himself?

Everyone is thinking the same, eyebrows raised in slight

mockery. Their teacher takes in their reactions and then grins back at his students. As usual, he knows exactly what he is doing.

'Guys, you may have noticed that I've got my tie on the wrong way round, and I guess you're wondering why. Well, I just wanted to show you that it is all right to get things wrong. Yes... *wrong*. You're all so scared of talking in these lessons, but you really don't need to be. Just remember the backwards tie and speak up a little more.'

The students laugh and lift their eyes from their desks. Eye contact is OK now, as wrong answers are fine. Every now and again, 12J still has awkwardly silent lessons—but, on the whole, the pressure to perform perfectly has vanished.

What God says

In this section of the chapter, I'm going to dig into what God says about the pressures you're facing. I'll use Bible passages to create a space in which you can reflect on and listen to God's words. Give yourself a quiet moment to prepare your heart: pray that you'll be open to hear what God has to say.

I mentioned previously that I'm applying to university this year. The process is long and complex, but, once the forms are sent in, all I can do is wait for the universities to respond, hoping that they will offer me a place. There are two types of offers. The first is conditional, giving me a place if I achieve particular A Level grades; the second is unconditional. An unconditional offer means that I'll be accepted at that university regardless of the grades I get at A Level. I could get two E grades and a U and still be accepted.

It's obvious which type of offer everyone hopes for. It's crazy not to want unconditional offers—offers with no 'if' clauses, catches or requirements, and consequently no pressure to achieve specific, often high, grades.

Just as we desire unconditional university offers, we often want to receive love that's unconditional. We want love that has no catches, no expectations and no pressures to be a certain way or do particular things. This can sound like a distant dream, when we actually experience people's love coming with expectations and requirements. When you think about it, your friends' love comes with the conditions that you must be nice to them always, buy them birthday presents and not gossip about them. If you don't live up to these expectations, arguments can arise, sometimes ending in broken friendships and a lack of love. This may be all too familiar and obvious to you, but it's true: the love we give and receive is often conditional.

I would suggest that what we want, and maybe even need, is love that accepts our messiness and flaws, offering forgiveness even when we make the biggest mistakes. But is there really such a thing as 'unconditional love'? Is there anyone who can truly love us without expectations or conditions?

If you're a Christian, you'll know that there is someone who does love us unconditionally. You'll know that this someone sees us in all our brokenness and mistakes, and yet still wraps his arms around us in infinite grace. This someone is Jesus, who is God.

Romans 5:8 says, 'God demonstrates his own love for us in this: while we were still sinners, Christ died for us.' This verse gives me goosebumps whenever I read it, as it describes truly unconditional and unlimited love. It's love that had our backs even while we were still turning from God; even while human beings hammered nails into Jesus' wrists, he still looked on us with love and breathed his last so that we sinners could breathe our first.

This means that God loves us not because of anything we have or haven't done. He loved us even before we realised that the man hanging from that cross was God himself. Nothing we can do can make God love us more, and, equally, nothing we can do can make him love us less. No school grade could possibly change the love that God has for us; none of it stops him from accepting us into his kingdom and loving us eternally.

This love really is eternal. In Jeremiah 31:3, God says, 'I have loved you with an everlasting love; I have drawn you with unfailing kindness.' God's love is constant, unchanging for all eternity. So even when everything around us seems shaky and uncertain, when we're thinking, 'Will I ever be clever enough for my teachers or classmates?', we know that God's love is the rock and promise on which we can stand. He will hold us through everything.

Just before my AS exams, I was super-nervous. Would I remember everything? Would I achieve the grades I needed? I knew that God loved me but still I was nervous. It's hard not to be when so much seems to hang on a couple of hours at a desk in an exam hall. About 15 minutes before one of my exams, I received an email from my godfather. It said:

Right—I am specifically praying right now that you don't fall asleep in your exam, crash to the ground and knock over the next person's desk, which then sends the rest toppling in a domino-like effect.

Be assured—I have no doubt that God will answer that prayer!

Oh, and I'll also pray you'll find inspiration, calm and contentment, safe in the knowledge that you're completely loved, whatever happens!

My godfather is an amazing, funny guy. But as well as providing me with some uplifting pre-exam humour, these words had a truly profound effect on me, as if my godfather's prayer was reaching through the screen of my phone and giving me a big, reassuring Jesus-hug.

The words 'safe in the knowledge that you're completely loved, whatever happens' are the words that got me through the rest of my exams. They encapsulate the great love of God expressed in 1 John 4:18, which reads, 'There is no fear in love. But perfect love drives out fear.' God's love is perfect and makes us fearless even when we're confronted with exams or struggles or bad days. It's a love that's complete and whole; we can go into every moment knowing that we are 'completely loved whatever happens'. Because of this, we can have confidence and contentment, even when we're in school. God's perfect love leaves no room for fear of failure or embarrassment or getting things wrong.

Ann Voskamp (one of my favourite writers) noticed that 'all fear is the lie that God's love ends'.[2] When we believe that God's love is not everlasting and doesn't constantly hold us, we allow fear to enter our hearts and begin to control our attitudes and actions. We reason that if God's love isn't always there for us, we need to get things exactly right in order to hold everything together for ourselves. A heart beating in fear expresses itself in a life lived in fear, stress and panic. This is a life so far from the fearless, love-filled life that God offers us in 1 John 4:18.

Accepting God's fearless love gives us the freedom not to be panicked or stressed, whether it's about schoolwork or anything else. When we know that we are accepted by God, no matter what, we are set free from the fear that cripples us and pushes us to try harder to be better or cleverer.

Hear this: God's love gives you the freedom to get things wrong, because he has got everything right already. It gives you the freedom to take risks, because God will always be there to catch you. It gives you the freedom to be weak, because God is strong enough for you.

Because of this overwhelming love of God, you can say that you've had enough of trying to be good or clever enough in school. Jesus is saying, 'Daughter, I have already done everything for you. You are loved and accepted already; you are already made enough in me.'

God's love gives us freedom just to be ourselves, without running around as if life is an emergency that we have to respond to and fix. In terms of the pressures of school and our future, God's love gives us the freedom not to have to achieve consistently high grades. God loves you whether you get 100 per cent or 0 per cent in those exams. There's always going to be a place for you to live your life, even without exam grades and a university degree: check out Jeremiah 29:11.

This security for our future, bound up in God's love, gives us the freedom to do our best, whether it reaches the standards of our schools and teachers or not. We no longer have the pressure of fabricating and directing our futures: God is the author of life's grand story, and you are a character in that story. It's God who holds the pen, not you, and he only asks that you trust him to write the words as you do your best to honour him, for he will make sure that you are exactly where he wants you to be.

My youth leader, Amy, showed me what it means to know that God is the author of her life. Her life-verse is the aforementioned Jeremiah 29:11: '"For I know the plans I have for you," declares the Lord, "plans to prosper you and not to harm you, plans to give you hope and a future."' Amy often shared with us the struggles she was facing, and demonstrated an amazing faith that God really was writing her story, so she didn't need to worry about whether she was good enough for the people around her.

This gave her freedom just to be herself, leaving behind the expectations and labels and pressures of being a youth worker. She taught me so much about being the person I am made to be; during one of our 'Costa chats' we realised something that totally transformed my outlook on life and faith: God made us as human *beings*, not human *doings*.

We so often act like human doings, people who have to keep busy and do things in order to be the best and hold life together. But really, we are human beings, created to be. We are here to 'be still, and know' that God is God (see Psalm 46:10). Knowing God's love gives us the freedom to be still, and to be human beings first. Out of our being flows our doing, because ultimately it is our being that is expressed in our doing; who we are inside is expressed by our external actions. Think about a smile: a smile is an external show of inward happiness, just as doing is an expression of our internal being.

'But Hannah,' you might say, 'I don't have time to be still! I have too much homework to do and people to see, and how on earth will I get it all done and not totally fail at life if I spend time just being still? Being still is not a practical option, however much my doing is meant to come from my being!'

Lovely girl, I often feel the same. Those question- and exclamation-marked sentences are exactly the sentences that dominated my mind throughout GCSE years, and they still return to haunt me. I have days when I come home from school and collapse on my bed, trying to motivate myself to start doing homework *that just needs to be perfect*, even if I really need to rest and be still first.

However, I have found that when I rest in God's love first, I am so much less stressed and panicked. I am still able to do all of the work I need to do. In fact, I am more productive when I take the time to breathe and still my pounding heart. Being still, paradoxically, is the secret to less stress, during everyday life as well as exams. Out of a connection with God that is found in the still moments flows our best living: the 'to do' list that you have waiting will be completed better when you let God love you first.

When we know God's great love for us, we are given freedom to be and to rest, to sink deep into the love of God and be recharged. To trust God's unconditional, everlasting, perfect, fearless and overcoming love is to slow down and take some deep breaths in the busyness of life, and to let our doing flow from our being instead of the other way around.

A final Bible passage I'd like to share with you is Romans 8:38–39: 'I am convinced that neither death nor life, neither angels nor demons, neither the present nor the future, nor any powers, neither height nor depth, nor anything else in all creation, will be able to separate us from the love of God.'

This, right here, is love that will never let you go. It's love that stretches from one end of the universe to the other, wrapping its arms around you, no matter how far you feel from God. This is love that means you never stop being God's daughter, whether you are at home, out with friends or in the exam hall.

As you read this book and live your life, remember that you are a daughter of the one true king who loves you so perfectly that nothing can ever separate you from him. Carry this love in your heart as you enter those tall metal gates early in the morning, and let it warm you from the inside out in the cold air. As those clamouring voices reach your ears, remember to listen out for God's still, small voice whispering love over your life, giving you freedom to be still and rest.

Headphones time

Spend some time now with metaphorical headphones on, blocking out the rest of the world and focusing only on God and your relationship with him. Use the questions below if it helps, or just spend some quiet time dwelling in God's love.

- Have you ever encountered stressful times because of school?
- What words or phrases would you choose to describe your thoughts at those times?
- How does it make you feel to know that God's love is unconditional, everlasting, perfect, fearless and overcoming?
- How could you build time into your day to 'be still and know' that God is God? Think about how you use your mornings and evenings, and how you could factor in some time to spend with God amid the routines and rhythms you have already in place.
- Read Psalm 46. Which words or phrases stand out to you? Why? Write them in your school planner or on notes to stick in places where you'll see them.

Soundtrack

'Rest' by Nevertheless.

Sometimes it can feel as if you have no time to rest when you have homework assignments and deadlines. But rest is essential; it's the foundation of your emotional, physical and spiritual well-being. Take time out to listen to this song and just be, resting in the grace that is God and is life.

3

Beautiful enough:
you are fearfully and wonderfully made

Every second of every day he pursues us and offers us grace, but until we take off our masks, we will never be able to accept it.

JEFFERSON BETHKE[3]

The big picture

Wake up. Stretch out, arms straightening. This duvet is warm, comfortable—maybe sleep a little longer? No. Feet hit floor, toes flexing. Stand up: commit to the day. Open blind, be blinded by sunrise light in return. Now I'm awake.

I walk over, grab a hairbrush and grin into the mirror: a dark mess of hair frames sleepy eyes. I brush out tangles and smooth stray hairs down, massaging my eyes with my free hand. I shower, and over the next 30 minutes I flit around my room, finding clothes, earrings, eyeliner, glancing always in the mirror to check my appearance—the combination of clothes, my hair.

Slowly, my look for the day forms, edges smoothed over as I scrutinise my reflection in that unforgiving, shiny plane of glass. I smile at myself when I'm done: I'm ready.

I guess you're familiar with this wake-up-and-prepare routine (unless you stay in bed all day—if that's you, I'm jealous). Days must start somewhere. Perhaps you sip a cup of hot tea as you pull on clothes, brush out hair and apply make-up. And I'm sure you're familiar with the confrontation that happens each morning—the face-off between yourself and your reflection.

You look yourself in the eye. What can you see there? Loneliness? Happiness? Then you look yourself up and down. Breathe in tight: 'This is what I'd look like if I were skinnier. If only…'. You then get right up close, exploring each inch of your face: 'Hmmm. Maybe I need to try a new face scrub. My skin's not as good as it could be. And a haircut is definitely needed soon. How should I wear my eyeliner today? What will people notice, but not too much?'

Think about what runs through your mind when you look in the mirror each morning. Have you ever had any 'if only' moments? Moments when you've thought 'If only I looked like…', 'If only I was…', 'If only I had those clothes…'?

These moments reveal something much deeper about how we think of ourselves, our image and the perceptions of other people. For the rest of this section, I'm going to uncover the meaning that lies behind our mirror confrontations, and what it could mean for our lives.

A few paragraphs previously, I described the mirror as 'unforgiving'. This is 'personification', talking about the mirror as if it's a person critiquing how I look. You may not know it, but that mirror over there on your wall is not just polished wood-framed glass. She's a person, a voice telling you what you need to change and how you need to change it. She rates your appearance and judges you honestly, revealing your flaws as well as your beauty.

We often, without realising it, treat mirrors like people. The reason we have those 'if only' moments when we see our reflection is because we see an imaginary 'someone else' there, judging who we are, based on how we look.

It's as if the mirror offers the first impression of you for the day. First impressions are important: they can shape the way a person views you, or even the way they behave towards you, for the rest of the time you know them. A first impression can get you a job; it can make you lifelong friends or it can set people against you. It's startling to realise that it only takes us two to seven seconds to form first impressions: people unconsciously make an assessment and form an opinion of you at the very moment you meet. So your appearance, both in looks and attitude, really is crucial, particularly when meeting someone for the first time.

This piles on a huge amount of pressure, don't you think? Herein lies one cause of the 'if only' moments—'If only I had nicer clothes/shinier hair…' or 'If only I looked prettier/skinnier/happier… other people would like me.'

A second cause is our tendency to make comparisons. In order to be dissatisfied with our appearance, we must have a standard to compare ourselves with, one that we believe we fail to meet. Each day we are bombarded with images of the 'ideal woman' who has the perfect figure, the shiniest hair and flawless make-up. Her clothes match brilliantly and she seems to want for nothing. This constantly reinforced image can become a standard that we strive continually to reach, believing that if we get there we will lack nothing and be accepted by all those around us.

Even if we don't compare ourselves with the images of women presented in the media and in advertising, we all compare ourselves with the real women we know and see around us each day—school peers, family members or leaders at church. Every day we get out our measuring sticks and line ourselves up against other people, comparing ourselves with the way *they* look.

The mirror's voice whispers again: 'You don't look as good as that popular girl at school. And that cousin of yours? Her clothes are so much nicer than yours. You're going to need to try harder to look pretty enough. If only you did this… you'd look as good as them.'

Here's another 'if only' moment—and you see that 'as good as' construction? That signals comparison, having an image in your mind that you strive to obtain. But, as Theodore Roosevelt said, 'Comparison is the thief of joy.'[4] Roosevelt was President of the USA over 100 years ago, and what he said then rings true for us now: comparing ourselves with others robs us of joy, disheartening us when we believe our image isn't as good as theirs.

A particularly prevalent form of comparison with others is related to the issue of weight, size or body shape. Maybe, for you, it isn't just the mirror that is unforgiving; perhaps the bathroom scales act as another judgemental voice. Weight can be a struggle, those numbers defining who we are, setting us up against the perfect weight, a standard reinforced by images in the media. We can feel disheartened when we don't measure up to that ideal, and sometimes this leads to more serious issues, such as depression and eating disorders. Having not struggled with these particular issues myself, any knowledge I have is second-hand, so I don't feel that I can talk about them as empathetically as I would like. If you are having a difficult time, there are people who can walk through it with you, more helpfully than I can. If you need someone to listen, book an appointment with your school nurse or doctor, confide in a friend or family member, or find out more on the NHS website.

Let's look at the word 'unforgiving' again. It may seem obvious, but scales and mirrors aren't actually unforgiving. They are not people; they're just inanimate objects with no feelings or opinions. They're the passive objects in our morning confrontations; *we* are the unforgiving ones.

We're so self-unforgiving because we're concerned about how people look at us—what their opinions are of our looks, actions, weight and behaviour. We fear the opinions they *could* have. What if they think I look silly? What if they think I'm not pretty enough? What will they think?

We're unforgiving towards ourselves because we care about the potentially unforgiving judgement of other people on our looks or attitude. However little we notice it, I would suggest that we all, in some way, care about how we compare with the 'ideal image', and this is all right, up to a point. It is definitely OK to want to look your best and present yourself in the best light.

But what about when it goes beyond that point? When our desire to present ourselves well becomes a striving to be the image of pure perfection, we become consumed by the fear that we won't be good enough if we don't look pretty enough.

This drives us to act differently about our image and appearance. If body size worries you, exercise and dieting may have begun to feature in your life. If you worry about your skin, perhaps make-up is your best friend. Whatever your struggle with image, think about your way of coping with that struggle. Does it have a positive or negative effect on how you view yourself?

While our morning preparations can be simply about

getting ready for the day, they can also become a time when we put on a mask to hide our true feelings. The mask might be make-up, particular clothes, a confident persona, all things that cover up the way we feel inside and what we perceive as our flaws. We dress to impress, to perform to a standard and win over others' approval. We believe the 'if onlys': 'If only you had better clothes/make-up/hair, you would be happier and more loved.' We act on these promises, hoping to achieve an appearance that's 'good enough'.

Do you ever feel like this? Do you think you're preparing not simply to be yourself for the day, but to be someone different—someone who people will like, accept, and love?

I read a blog called *A Girl Like Me*. In September 2014, the blogger posted a piece called 'Keeping up appearances'. These were some of the words from that post: 'Masks don't take away our pain and struggle... they just cover it up.'[5]

It's so true. While self-image may not be an immediate problem to you, I would suggest that we all face times where we put on masks to hide our true feelings and insecurities. We put on masks as we look in the mirror each morning, so that we can step through the day knowing that *at least* the way we look externally is OK. *At least* people will approve of me and like me. We accept the promise of the 'if only' and we put on our masks, believing that it will all turn out better, and we will be pretty enough for others' approval.

But this performance of communicating that we are OK, that we've got it all together, is exactly that—a performance, enacted on each day's stage. And after the curtains go down at the end of the show, we slump, unseen by the audience. When we're alone, the masks come off, and we get real again. Then we realise that this charade is exhausting.

The close-up

Do you feel as if you're the only one who struggles with image and beauty? You're not. Have a read of the two stories below and reflect on what and who they are about. Before you read, I want to mention that, although these two stories both involve boys as the catalyst for the pressure on image, guys are not the only source of expectation. Think about what else could encourage a negative self-image—perhaps family, friends, movies, music, or yourself.

I began to read *King Lear* in the peaceful quiet of the canteen, settling down for an hour's study. Then, noise arrived.

'So who would *you* rate as the top five girls in our year, then?' Tom had come in, taking his place at a nearby table, others joining him as they overheard his words.

Steve responded with more questions: 'Ooohhhh, I dunno... What are we going on? Looks? Personality? Intelligence?'

'Looks, of course! I mean, that's the most important, right?' Tom laughed as he spoke, half-jokingly choosing the most superficial, yet most popular, topic.

'OK... so... Jemima, then Katherine, then maybe Megan...? They're all pretty fit. If Katherine was a bit taller, she'd be *perfect*!'

Tom's voice rose above the murmurs of agreement: 'You're going for the classics, then?'

'Yeah, I mean, they're the best looking in our year, by far. Everyone knows that.'

('The classics', I later discovered, were the people most often rated within the top five of our year group.)

Rosie joined the discussion. 'How about Ashley? If I were a guy, I'd definitely ask her out. Top quality girlfriend material right there!'

'Great choice! Oh, Rosie, you missed out on *all* the fun yesterday. We discussed basically everyone in the year—who looks best and who needs improvements. You should have been there, it was great!'

So the conversation continued. I was close to furious. I wanted to ask them, 'Please have a little more respect for these girls you're rating; how do you think they'd feel if they heard your conversation?' Intimidated, I kept quiet. Regrettably, having had a vivid insight into how these people rated others' appearance, I feared what they thought of me. Despite knowing that their opinion of my image didn't really matter, I felt an enormous amount of pressure to look just like their description of the 'perfect girl'.

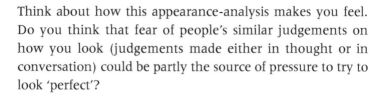

Think about how this appearance-analysis makes you feel. Do you think that fear of people's similar judgements on how you look (judgements made either in thought or in conversation) could be partly the source of pressure to try to look 'perfect'?

Why here? Now? Today? Why me? Him? Us? Well, not 'us'. Just me, now, pushed into perpetual loneliness by the poison that overspilled from his heart straight into mine. The questions look back at me as my tear-drenched eyes gaze into the mirror: I think, in my brokenness, that I am the answer. He cheated on me because I am not good enough—not pretty enough, not clever enough, not thin enough.

His caustic words grow wild in my mind, even though he is gone. The words expand, fill my thoughts and foster self-hate, like ivy springing up around the sinews of my heart, the leaves covering and choking the spark of my personality, in which I was once so confident. I am forced into something new.

As I turn away from the mirror, my eyes fall on the scales. Maybe this could be a solution...

Days wear on and I try to become acceptable, perfect, lovable. The numbers fall lower on the scales—but are they low enough? Will I *ever* be good enough?

As these thoughts circle and months pass, I slowly retreat into myself, the ivy becoming the controlling mask of my new personality. And then, some hope? Some love? Has someone noticed me?

Even better: someone has noticed not only the ivy-me, but the real me. Someone has noticed that spark, which had nearly gone out, and he cherishes it. This time, he is lovely, loving, true.

Even greater: the unconditional love of God sees the spark, too. He is reviving it, gently blowing on the embers and fanning them into flame, the orange heat burning away the leaves surrounding my heart. Although I still struggle daily with anxiety, and still dress to fit in, impress and be perfect, God sees the 'me' beneath it all, and he is loving me back to life.

What God says

We've all heard the cliché, 'It's what's inside that counts', used pervasively in advertising, on TV and in everyday conversations. It's a statement that can have a variety of purposes—to empower people who feel unappreciated; to sell a product; to act as a reminder of what is really important. Do you know where this cliché came from? A quick internet search doesn't answer the question, and beyond the internet I'm not sure where to start looking. However, I would suggest that it originates from the Bible, or at least that it bears a strong resemblance to the message the Bible gives.

Open up a Bible and read 1 Peter 3:3–5. I love the way Peter writes of beauty here, speaking directly about the emphasis that our mirror-confrontations place on our external appearance. The way *THE MESSAGE* paraphrases verse 3 is particularly challenging and inspiring: 'What matters is not your outer appearance—the styling of your hair, the jewellery you wear, the cut of your clothes—but your inner disposition.' *It's what's inside that counts.*

Peter pinpoints the source of your beauty as who you are on the inside. In other words, it's your character and attitude that make you beautiful. These are things that the mirror doesn't reveal; a pane of glass can't look into and reflect your innermost being, your heart.

Peter isn't the only man in the Bible who had this insight into true beauty. You may know of David, the famous king of Israel, whose life is documented in the Old Testament. God chose David to fulfil the role of king: he sent Samuel to anoint David as King Saul's reign was drawing to a close. David's father was Jesse, and Jesse had seven sons older than David, all of whom he paraded in front of Samuel. Surely one of these strapping young lads would be God's chosen king? They were all handsome, strong, popular… what's not to like? At least, these were the thoughts that Samuel had when he met the eldest of Jesse's sons, Eliab.

However, God quickly spoke to Samuel: 'Do not consider his appearance or his height, for I have rejected him. The Lord does not look at the things people look at. People look at the outward appearance, but the Lord looks at the heart' (1 Samuel 16:7). Here we see it again: *it's what's inside that counts.*

Samuel had seen the good, kingly looks of Eliab and

assumed that God had chosen him as king, but he couldn't see right into the depths of Eliab's heart—what motivated him, how he behaved, what his character was truly like. Only God could, and God saw that Eliab didn't have the qualities fit for a leader. In fact, God chose the shepherd-boy, Jesse's youngest and almost forgotten son who had stayed behind to tend the sheep as Samuel arrived. He wasn't considered good enough to be a king, yet, as David approached, God spoke again to Samuel: 'Rise and anoint him; this is the one' (v. 12). God looked into David's heart and saw a ruler.

You see again the emphasis on the inside, the heart, the inner disposition. God looked straight past the outward appearance and saw what mattered most. The heart of the matter is truly the matter of the heart; *it's what's inside that counts*.

Does this mean that God is asking us not to care about how we look, and instead to wear no make-up, never style our hair and wear whatever clothes we find in our rooms? I used to think that the answer to this question was 'yes'. I believed that I should pay as little attention as possible to my image; I should wear clothes that fitted and looked all right, but not care too much about them.

Times have changed, however! My view of beauty and image has shifted since discovering Peter's words and the story of David's anointing. I don't believe that God wants us just to forget about image and appearance; after all, he created our bodies and the entire concept of beauty. Beauty and image, like most things, aren't inherently bad, and being beautiful is not something that Christians shouldn't care about. Rather, if we view beauty as God does, our perceptions are transformed. We see that beauty isn't a performance we have to put on to hide our true identity, but that true beauty is to do with our inner disposition. Our image on the outside is truly beautiful when it reflects the beauty that hums on the inside of us. Our outside image can be an expression of who we are inside, and that is a beautiful thing.

Pete Greig's prophetic poem 'The vision' draws a clear contrast between our outside and our inside. The poem talks of 'an army of young people' who 'are incredibly cool, dangerously attractive inside'. They are living and loving for Jesus on the inside, but 'On the outside? They hardly care. They wear clothes like costumes to communicate and celebrate but never to hide.'[6] (For the rest of the poem, visit www.24-7prayer.com/thevisionpoem. I definitely recommend it. Go read and be changed!)

I love the phrase 'costumes to communicate and celebrate but never to hide'. Greig exactly encapsulates what the Bible says about beauty and image. Our outside image should not be a mask that hides our inside identity; it should be an extension of our inside beauty, celebrating our identity in Christ and communicating our love for Jesus. With this, there's no pressure to look a particular way or wear particular clothes, just a freedom to make choices about your outside image based on your identity as God's beautiful daughter.

This is how Esther used her image. Esther has her own book in the Bible, telling the story of how she was chosen to be the wife of King Xerxes, a circumstance that led her to save the Jewish people in the Persian kingdom. The process of becoming Xerxes' wife was a long one, involving 'twelve months of beauty treatments... six months with oil of myrrh and six with perfumes and cosmetics' (Esther 2:12). She also had to hide the fact that she was a Jew (v. 10).

I couldn't begin to imagine having a whole year in intensive beauty school, but this was Esther's life, and it was her image that was pleasing to Xerxes and enabled her to become his wife. As soon as she gained this royal position, she used her influence powerfully to save the Jews from a death order.

So here we see image and beauty used as tools to achieve God's plans and purposes. Esther's beauty placed her in Xerxes' palace 'for just such a time as this' (4:14, NLT). It can be the same for us, our image being a part of who we are for God.

Esther could do all of this because she was fully secure in her identity in God. Even though God is not mentioned once in the book of Esther, we can see in her courageous actions that she trusted him completely, saying, as she approached Xerxes with her request for the Jews to be saved, 'If I perish, I perish' (4:16). Esther knew deep within her that she was safe in God's arms, and so, on the outside, her image was an overspill of her confidence and hope in God. True God-inspired beauty comes from a beauty on the inside that only stems from security and contentment in our identity in Christ. We return to where we began: *it's what's inside that counts*.

But what if, on the inside, you don't feel beautiful or secure? What if you feel shaky, confused or lost? I have been through times when I've felt completely broken inside, unlovable and lost in a world where I couldn't tell where my heart was rooted. Sometimes it's a real struggle to remember who I am. In the words of Shakespeare's King Lear, I find myself asking, 'Who is it that can tell me who I am?'[7]

I love this question. It's so searching, and it prompts us to go deeper than we thought we could, in search of our roots and our identity. Notice that Lear uses the word 'who'. He's asking 'who' he can find his identity in, not 'what' or

43

'where'. Here, I see King Lear's realisation that wealth, land and riches can't ever define who he is, because these things change. I see him beginning to understand that the things of this world can never satisfy us or give us true worth and identity. It is only a person who can give us these answers.

For Lear, this 'person' was his own shadow, a recollection of his former days as a glorious king, before he grew old and mad. For us as Christians, this person is Jesus.

Do you know the verse 'Whoever wants to save their life will lose it, but whoever loses their life for me and for the gospel will save it'? It's recorded in Mark 8:35, and it is Jesus speaking to his disciples. It's potentially a confusing verse, but I think it's a real encouragement and challenge for us to let go of all of the things in life that we think are important, all the things that we think will make us good enough, all the things we think will bring us true, lasting identity. When we do let go of these things, we will 'save', or find, our life—our true self. And we will find it in Jesus, as we let go of our striving to look as if we're holding life together, and let God shape us with his love and grace. When we realise that our efforts to be perfect and beautiful are never going to be enough, we let God be our 'enough' for us, giving us a firm identity on the inside that spills out as true beauty.

Take a look at these verses. This is what God says about who you are.

- God 'chose us in [Christ] before the creation of the world to be holy and blameless in his sight' (Ephesians 1:4).
- You are 'fearfully and wonderfully made' (Psalm 139:14).
- You are God's 'treasured possession' (Exodus 19:5).
- In God 'we live and move and have our being' (Acts 17:28).

- God loves you just as he loves his Son, Jesus (see John 17:23).
- Nothing at all 'will be able to separate us from the love of God' (Romans 8:39).
- You are God's 'masterpiece' (Ephesians 2:10, NLT).
- 'Christ has truly set us free' (Galatians 5:1, NLT).
- You are made who you are 'for just such a time as this' (Esther 4:14, NLT).

The Bible is like an epic love letter from God to his people, of which you are one. This is how he sees you—as a treasure, a beauty. Just like he did with David, God sees past all your masks, all your fears and insecurities, and all the thoughts other people have about you. He sees past it all and straight into your heart, your inner disposition. There he sees the beauty he placed humming at your core, and he declares you his beautiful daughter.

In his book *What's So Amazing About Grace?* Philip Yancey asks this question: 'How would my life change if I truly believed the Bible's astounding words about God's love for me, if I looked in the mirror and saw what God sees?'[8]

Looking in the mirror and seeing yourself as God sees you is amazingly transformative. Instead of believing the mirror's hissing voice when it says, 'You are just not good enough... no one will ever love *you*', you can drown those words out with the roar of God's love. Instead of hiding from people who might judge you for who you are, you can show your true self, safe in the knowledge that God sees you as beautiful, his own.

God's still, small voice sings love over your soul: be encouraged and begin to take off those masks! Stop performing, and let people see the transformation that Jesus is working in your heart, bringing out your best beauty and setting you truly free.

Headphones time

We've discussed much about image and beauty in this chapter, perhaps touching some issues that you have been thinking through or struggling with. Spend some time now in a quiet space, listening to God's voice amid the busyness. You could revisit some of the Bible stories and passages mentioned (1 Peter, the story of David in 1 Samuel, and Esther) or use the pointers below if it helps to direct your thinking and prayer time.

- Think of three words that your friends or family would use to describe you. Are they the words that you would use to describe yourself?
- Are there any areas of your life in which you wear a 'mask'? Does it ever feel as if no one knows the real you? Why?
- Are you secure in your identity on the inside? Do you know you're beautiful? God sees the depths of who you are and the beauty he placed right at your core. Take a few minutes to reflect on these words from Psalm 139:13–16: 'For you created my inmost being; you knit me together in my mother's womb. I praise you because I am fearfully and wonderfully made; your works are wonderful, I know that full well. My frame was not hidden from you when I was made in the secret place, when I was woven together in the depths of the earth. Your eyes saw my unformed body.'

- How does it make you feel to know that God sees you as his beautiful daughter? How can this transform the way you view your image and your identity?
- Grab a felt-tip pen and write on your mirror the one verse or word that will remind you of your identity in Jesus. (Don't worry, felt-tip rubs off mirrors!)

Soundtrack

'Beautiful things' by Gungor.

As you listen, reflect on what, or rather who, it is that makes you beautiful and sees your beauty as more than good enough. How does this make you feel? What encouragement does it give you?

Humility's enough:
coping with friendship group conflict

Our specific offerings reveal the unique variety of our worship, not for the glory of us, but to the glory of God and the benefit of others.

EMILY P. FREEMAN[9]

The big picture

She sat there, huddled into the back of the sofa, waiting for the evening to end. When would they leave? She'd only invited a few of her girlfriends over from church for an evening of pizza and movies. It had all been going brilliantly, with all of them chattering over the action flick they'd put on the TV. But a sudden tension had built up in the room, as if there were strings between them that had all been pulled taut, stretched to breaking point. And it was all because of a few misplaced comments from Rosie. 'You know, Georgie, you really need to vary your wardrobe a bit more. You always wear the same two dresses, and, like, it's a bit boring.' Or even 'Kate, would you like to come over to mine? I could teach you how to paint properly.' Kate was top of her class for art, and Rosie hadn't even noticed that she'd offended anyone. But now it was there—the tension, the strings stretched and ready to snap.

How would this all play out in the next few weeks? Would there be rumours and gossip? Or just one explosive shouting match? Yes, there can be arguments in church youth groups. She just wished the night was over already, before the strings broke.

━━━━━ ▫️▪️▫️ ━━━━━

We all love our friends. We share the best moments of our life with them—celebrations, school times, days out and nights in, time spent relaxing, working together and supporting each other. Our friends are a massive part of our lives: we live with them, love with them and laugh with them. They are the people that know us the best and know how to make us happy.

But what about when it all goes wrong? What about when our relationships with friends are not so idyllic? We have all experienced moments of frustration with the people we value most. We engage in arguments about the smallest irritations and misunderstandings, and even though, in retrospect, we may see that the problem was really small and insignificant, at the time it can feel like a war zone. Voices are raised, verbal revenge is rampant and tempers run high. Eventually, one of you gives in, or you both do, but after the argument you still feel the pain of the abrasive words that you both received and sent. Hatred can be harboured in hearts for weeks, and you can be internally angry with your friends for months.

You may also be familiar with a subtler kind of warfare. Arguments flourish when secrets, lies and gossip spring up among us, and as hatred and frustration take root in our hearts. We find ourselves whispering behind each other's backs, maintaining that we are right even as we destroy each other with manipulation and tactical comments. We may not even realise we're doing it, but often we are so tangled up in the argument that we become a part of the problem instead of the solution.

On the surface, this 'war zone' analogy seems like an exaggeration, but conflict between friends really does cause casualties. Whether you end up with an irreparable relationship or division within a friendship group, there is always a reminder of the bullets that were fired. Anger can linger for days, weeks or even months, and hatred can take a painful grip on our hearts, leaving visible marks on our lives. Conflict hurts, and is a reality in each of our lives; even if we are not a direct part of conflict, we may know people who are.

I'm sure we can all remember the anger and hurt we have felt due to disagreements. Think about one of those times for a moment. It could have been about anything, big or small; just picture that time in your head.

What was it that made you frustrated? Maybe it was because the other person 'just didn't understand', or perhaps it was because they 'just never listen' and 'always have something against you'. The thing that makes me most frustrated is when no one will agree with me even though I am *most definitely right*!

Arguments arise in situations where two people with conflicting opinions or interests both believe that they are either right or more important. The people in this situation compete for the victory of 'being right'; whatever the cost, they argue passionately for their viewpoint. This desire for and dedication to the goal of 'being right' can come from different places, but, in friendships, I think it is because we all feel as if we are inadequate, or not as good as others, and are all looking for a way to feel more adequate, accepted and approved. It's similar to school grades: we're all looking to achieve A grades in coolness, popularity and social success.

The bottom line is that we all want to be loved and valued, and somewhere inside each of us there is a fear of not being accepted.

When we feel that we are not as good as our friends, we can begin to fear that we are not good enough to be accepted by them. Instead of being ourselves, we try to be better so that they will like us and let us be a part of their friendship group.

Born out of this feeling of inadequacy and the fear of not being accepted are jealousy and competitiveness. They are the result of wanting to be as good as, or better than, the friends we have around us. We can be jealous of our friends' talents. Maybe one of your friends is an excellent public speaker and you get nervous every time you have to talk in front of people. You just want to be able to speak as well as your friend, and so you become jealous of what they can do. This jealousy can quickly turn into competition, and, without your friend even noticing, you can begin to try to be better than them; maybe you even start putting your friend down and gossiping about them. Either way, this can lead to conflict and hurt.

In a free period at school one day, I was chatting to some friends about a tricky situation they were going through in their friendship group. It was complex and confusing, and the emotions they both felt as the result of the conflict were draining. They laughed about the situation, but underneath the smiles there was real struggle and awkwardness.

I asked them, 'What do you think is the root cause of the conflict?' Their answer surprised me. I didn't expect to hear what I did from two girls who were obviously finding things difficult. They were self-critical, and they were fully aware of the problem.

They explained to me that everyone feels inadequate, so they try to make themselves feel better by putting others down. They said that, in arguments, each person becomes like an animal with a bad leg; an injured animal will attack the other animals so that it is not seen as the weakest. This continues on and on, each person scrambling to be the least weak. At each attack, everyone is brought lower and lower in a downward spiral caused by a desire to move upwards.

It's so true: in conflict, we are like wounded animals. We lash out at others, trying to protect ourselves from more pain, hiding inadequacy and insecurity behind harsh words and actions, and injuring others in the hope that we won't be the weakest person, the person who is left out.

When our acceptance is at stake, we hunger to see other people fall lower than us, so that we feel better about ourselves. This is how conflict is caused; when we don't feel as if we're good enough, we compete to hide our insecurities and expose the weaknesses of others so that we feel stronger.

When we look at situations of conflict in this way, it seems really ugly. Surely *I'm* not like that? Surely *I* don't act in this way? To be honest, these are the questions that I have been asking while writing this chapter. God, do I *really* have such a messy heart?

I believe I do, sometimes. I let myself be consumed by my feelings of inadequacy, and this drives me to act in hurtful pride against those closest to me. It *is* an ugly thing, revealing the broken nature of hearts not trusting fully in God. But I am glad I'm not the only one who has a messy heart like this. Looking close up, we can see that we all, really, let our insecurities and fears get hold of us more than they should.

The close-up

These are all stories of arguments that have really happened to people I know. Maybe these stories will describe something similar to situations you've been in, or maybe they'll just be useful for you to read, to let you know that you're not the only one. Perhaps you could grab a pen and some paper and scribble down a conflict-story of your own, something that you've been through or are going through. Let the words become your space for reflecting on your frustration, letting the hurt find vent through the ink flowing on to the page.

This story of conflict between friends illustrates how competing to be 'right' can be so wrong for relationships. It began in a pre-Year 7 choir, where two girls became Best Friends Forever. A few years later they formed a team for the Duke of Edinburgh award—an award, as you may know, involving a two-night camping expedition in which you have to navigate your way to each campsite using only a map and a compass. It requires a lot of teamwork. When these two girls returned to school after the expedition, everyone in the year quickly noticed that they no longer talked to each other, each gravitating towards a completely different friendship group. They had argued on the expedition, after getting lost, about who should read the map and who had got them lost in the first place. They both asserted that they were the better map reader of the two and they competed stubbornly for the victory of being right. By the end of the trip they had broken their friendship completely, and still, four years later, they have never spoken—or, at least, they have avoided each other as far as is possible in school.

A second story reached its climax with a shouting match across the foyer in school. Well, maybe it wasn't quite shouting—but I remember raised voices, angry faces and an ending that left the two of us storming out to form time in a high temper, defending wounded hearts. Yes, I was one of the people nearly shouting. I don't exactly remember the details, but I know that the tension had been building up for weeks, the smallest irritations causing friction between myself and someone with whom I've always had, let's say, a bit of an 'on/off' friendship.

This friend and I haven't always seen eye-to-eye on points of view or ways of dealing with circumstances. We are both quite stubborn and quick to defend our opinions, particularly if we feel that the other has begun to get the upper hand in a situation or is becoming more popular in our friendship group. We have argued over situations, other people, issues related to faith and God, and even just turns of phrase, utterances that were meant as jokes but were taken too seriously. This has often led us to take little digs at one another, disguising really harsh comments as jokes or light-hearted teasing.

I'm not proud of the way I've acted in these situations with my friend, however much she's annoyed or unintentionally hurt me. I have allowed rivalry and competition to stop me loving this friend as Jesus would. I've forgotten to see her as a person and perceived her more as an obstacle in my way.

With the perfection of hindsight, I can see that the way I treated her prevented me from sharing the real nature of God's love and grace with her and with all of my friends. Conflict can seem the only option, but, in reality, I *chose* to act out of the same insecurity and jealousy that fracture too many friendships.

(In case you were wondering, my friend and I get on a lot better now we've learned to love a little better. We no longer have raised-voice conversations in the middle of school!)

What God says

In the Bible it says that as God's children we are ambassadors of peace (see 2 Corinthians 5:18–20). We are the peacemakers mentioned in Matthew 5:9, blessed as sons and daughters of God because we keep the peace between people. One biblical word for 'peace' is *shalom*, which literally means 'completeness, soundness, welfare'.[10] Do you see the contrast between our identity as God's children and the reality of life? We, like everyone, cause conflict instead of bringing peace, fragmenting friendships and isolating people instead of promoting wholeness. In the midst of arguments, we become unsettled and forget our peaceful purpose.

God has a different way for us to live. He bestows on us an identity that removes our inadequacies and instead gives us confidence and peace within ourselves. In doing this, he allows us to let go of the struggle to be better than our friends and helps us to be humble instead, acting as the peacemakers in our friendship groups. To explore this new way of 'doing friendships', we are going to look at Matthew 18:15–20. Give this passage a read before we begin. Pray that God will open up your heart to him so that he can show you his words.

Verse 15 says, 'If your brother or sister sins against you, go and point out their fault, just between the two of you.' The opening verse to this passage begins with a reference to conflict—a 'brother or sister sinning against you'. This could mean any argument, irritation or conflict between you and a friend. You might even be the one to have caused it. When the conflict has started, it is easy to begin to gossip about your friend and what they have said or done that has hurt you. Even if you gossip in the context of asking someone for help, you can easily find yourself complaining about the person you have argued with. I know that I do this. If I feel wronged by someone, it's not long before I'm complaining about them behind their back.

Why do you think we do this? I would argue again that it's because we all like to be right. We always like to have the upper hand in a situation and to be elevated above the person who has hurt us, often portraying ourselves as the victim. We lift ourselves up by putting the other person down, perhaps by telling others 'just how bad they've been', and this worsens the relationship and isolates people. In verse 15, Jesus gives us another way to respond to being hurt in an argument. He doesn't say, 'Go and make yourself feel better by putting the other person down.' Instead he says, 'Point out their fault, *just between the two of you.*' At this stage, Jesus says that we should go and talk to the friend who has hurt us; chances are that they may not even have realised how hurt you are and all you need to do is to let them know. This approach to conflict means that you don't gossip about them; instead you talk humbly to them, saying, 'Hey, I felt hurt after our argument. Can we talk about it?'

Already we are taking steps towards peace and wholeness in friendships by laying down our pride, allowing ourselves to be authentic and vulnerable, opening the way to humble conversation about the problem.

Verse 16 says, 'If they will not listen, take one or two others along.' This verse tells us what to do when just talking to your friend doesn't work. Maybe they won't listen to what you have to say (or maybe you won't listen to them) and the conflict is made worse rather than better. If this happens, Jesus still doesn't give us permission to go up in arms and make ourselves feel better by gossiping to everyone we know. Instead, he suggests that we bring in only one or two trusted others who can act as witnesses. This means that they can evaluate the situation as they see it and help you to resolve the conflict. After all, 'we' is better than 'I' and collaboration like this can help you and your friend to see from each other's perspectives, learning to listen, compromise and move forwards.

Verse 17 says, 'If they still refuse to listen, tell it to the church; and if they refuse to listen even to the church, treat them as you would a pagan or a tax collector.' This verse can be split into two parts. The first part suggests that if the conflict still isn't resolved, even with one or two others helping, you should tell the church. This may be appropriate in some situations, but let's be real: if the conflict is between you and some friends at school, perhaps approaching your pastor/vicar/church leader to ask if they could tell your church about it on Sunday is not such a good idea. However, it can be useful to talk to someone from outside the conflict, who is in your church—maybe a youth leader—as they can help you to think about the situation in a different way.

The second part of the verse is the part that I find really interesting. It says, 'If [the friend who's hurt you] refuses to listen even then, treat them as you would a pagan or a tax collector.' This sounds very 'un-Jesus-like' at first glance. Is Jesus saying that we should treat the people with whom we argue as outcasts, as the Jewish people would have treated tax collectors and pagans in biblical times? Is that really a true reflection of Jesus' radical love? Some may argue that it is, that treating people as outsiders humbles them and makes them see their mistakes. However, I disagree: isn't that just another way of elevating yourself by putting them down? So, I would say that this verse means something quite different.

Ask yourself this: how did Jesus treat pagans and tax collectors? While the religious authorities looked down on tax collectors, *Jesus invited them to dinner*—or rather, he invited himself to dinner. Take the example of Zacchaeus, the man who literally climbed a tree to see Jesus. This man was a tax collector and was regarded as a 'sinner' by the other people around him, so when Jesus noticed Zacchaeus and said, 'I must stay at your house today', he was doing something very countercultural, something no one expected of the prophesied Messiah.

Going back to Matthew 18, we can see that Jesus is suggesting that we invite the person we are arguing with to our home for dinner. This seems ridiculous! Surely inviting that girl you have held a grudge against for months is just a recipe for disaster, not for a delicious meal? Actually, I think it's not so ridiculous. As Jesus dined with Zacchaeus, he removed the labels 'sinner' and 'tax collector' from Zacchaeus and spent time with him simply as a person loved and created by God. We can do the same. In the midst of conflict, it can be easy to lose sight of the fact that the person you're arguing with is a person, a human being just like you, created and loved by the same God who made you. So, inviting them to your house for food can begin to remove the labels that you have given them, and you can begin to see them once again as the friend you liked. In this way, conflict can be worked through as friends, with more respect and love for each other.

Not only does this action continue to move you towards peace; it also humbles you greatly, making you extend a hand of friendship and forgiveness even if you felt hurt or wronged. If we think about it, Jesus humbled himself when he stayed at Zacchaeus' house. Zacchaeus, in stealing money, had actually sinned against God, but Jesus was still willing to spend time with him. To follow Jesus' example of humility is to realise that we don't have to strive to be better than our friends, or strive to win the argument. Instead, humility brings peace and wholeness into our relationships as we lift our friends up and stop competing.

Verse 20 says, 'For where two or three come together in my name, there am I with them' (NIV 1984). You've probably heard this final verse of our passage in church, when someone is talking about a prayer meeting or time of worship. However, as it appears at the end of a passage that discusses conflict, I think it means something different. I think that Jesus is making us a promise here. He promises that whenever we come together to build *shalom*, whenever we live out our identity as ambassadors for peace, Jesus will be alongside us, helping us. What could be better than that?

Have you noticed the attitude that underlies this whole passage in Matthew 18? It's humility. Humility is one of those biblical ideas that can be hard to understand and even harder to live out in practice. It is the attitude of realising that the world isn't about you: it's all about God. It is the attitude of becoming lower, smaller—and, even though that may seem negative, it is actually a marvellously freeing attitude to live by. When we live humbly, bowing our knee to God, God lifts us up: 'Blessed are the meek, for they will inherit the earth' (Matthew 5:5). Being 'meek' is akin to being 'humble'; they're both associated with gentleness, with lowering oneself. In fact, 'humble' comes from the Latin *humus*, meaning 'earth'. How much lower can you get?

Ann Voskamp writes, 'In the upside down kingdom of heaven, down is up and up is down, and he who wants to ascend higher must descend lower.'[11] This paradoxical-looking statement captures the essence of humility: humility is the realisation that God is greater than me, and that that is more than OK.

Humility allows us to rest in the knowledge that we don't have to be the best: that's not our job. Humility frees us to say, 'I've had enough of trying to be good enough, of trying to scramble to a higher, better place. Instead, I'm going to step down completely, descending lower so that I can lift up my friends.' A passage that captures this idea perfectly is Philippians 2:3–4, which says, 'Do nothing out of selfish ambition or vain conceit. Rather, in humility value others above yourselves, not looking to your own interests but each of you to the interests of the others.' Ultimately, humility frees us so that we can see the value of other people, as Jesus did when he sat down for dinner with Zacchaeus. Valuing others leads us to lift them up, not put them down, promoting the wholeness-peace of *shalom* in our friendship groups, bringing out the best in each other and giving the message that each of the people in the friendship group is good enough, loved and accepted.

If we all stoop low to lift each other up, God too will be lifted up on this earth, as his peacemaker children glorify him with their living. Instead of seeing a downward spiral caused by an upward struggle, we will see an upward lifting caused by a downward bowing as we humble ourselves before God.

But how exactly do we humble ourselves? The art of humility is elusive, not coming easily to our proud and stubborn hearts. I would suggest that humility comes from realising that by yourself you can't be good enough, and you need God's grace to help you. Humility means holding out your empty hands for God to grab hold of and pull you up, by his strength and grace, not your own work. It's letting go of your inadequacies and fears, abandoning them to a God who will always be enough.

That's difficult. It's akin to a trust exercise where you have to fall backwards into someone's arms—it's terrifying! You wonder, 'Will they really catch me?' But Jesus promises that he will always be there to catch us, to guide us and help us. The God of the universe holds us close and will be with us in our conflicts, however small or large they are. What an encouragement that is! Even if being a peacemaker in your friendship group means that you are not seen as the 'winner' of the argument or the 'best' person, you can still work to bring peace, safe in the knowledge that Jesus will be with you and he will always be enough.

Headphones time

In this chapter you've read a lot about competitiveness, conflict and the healing power of a humble heart. It might have spoken into a situation that you're currently in, perhaps hitting a bit too close to home. Or you might not have experienced anything like this at all. Either way, use this time now to put some headphones on and listen just to God's voice. Perhaps read over Matthew 18:15–20 again, and sink into the words. Pray over what has stood out to you or challenged you.

You can use these questions to help you:

- What conflict have you encountered with your friends, either currently or in the past?
- What caused this conflict? Think about how you felt, and what was happening in your heart.
- How did you deal with the situation? You could have reacted in retaliation, with pride and anger, or acted

peacefully and gracefully. Be honest in your reflection. How did your reaction make you feel?

- How could Jesus' words from Matthew 18 help you to face problems with friends in the future? What practical actions can you take away from the example he sets?
- Think of a friend who you argue with. How can you lift them up and encourage them in what they're doing? Pray for them.

Soundtrack

'Losing' by Tenth Avenue North.

Reflect on the words of the song. When we follow Jesus' example regarding conflict and arguments, are we really losing, or are we learning to live humbly in the knowledge that we don't need to be the best?

5

Accepted as enough: letting your family see beneath the masks

In spite of the way that Israel had treated him, God's love for his stubborn child remained as intense as ever.

RAY MARKHAM[12]

The big picture

My dad is currently researching our family tree. So far, he's discovered who our relations were, all the way back to the 1500s; there's a possible poet, a large group of servants and even a criminal. Although they're super-distant relations, they are still regarded as 'family'. Yet, as I don't have a time machine, I cannot properly know them. Were they generous? Mean? Respected? Respectful?

Nor can I know how they lived as families. Did they argue or get on well? Were they considered 'normal' or did they have eccentricities? Were there secrets surrounding their households? I'll never know the answers to these questions, just as the likes and hates of each person will remain a mystery. It's fun to imagine their lives, but I can never know them as I know my family today.

Today, my family doesn't consist of poets, servants and

criminals (as far as I know!). In my family I have an aunt who's a teacher, a mum who works for a charity and a grandad who organises funerals. Yet I know far more about them than just their occupations. I know how my family works—what holds us together, what annoys each person, what we enjoy doing. So family can be defined in terms of the people we know well, those who we spend time with and live with, regardless of whether we're biologically related.

I don't know anything about your family. Maybe you're like me, living with your parents and siblings. Perhaps you're an only child. Maybe you don't live with your family, for whatever reason. You may not know one or both of your parents; you might be living with grandparents or a step-parent or other relations. I don't know, but I'm guessing that you have somewhere to call home and someone to share it with—your family.

Although our families are different, I hope that within our families we are all encouraged, built up and given a space to be ourselves. Family, I've found, can bring out the best in you, as they challenge and inspire you to live in the best way you can. I know that without my parents and sister encouraging me, I would not be sitting here writing this book for you.

As well as the good times, I would also suggest that we all experience family conflicts, feeling the pressures that come with family life. You might feel as if you're not good enough to be a part of your own family; perhaps you're under a lot of pressure to behave a certain way or achieve particular goals. Do you sometimes feel as if 'home' is synonymous with 'pressure', and 'family' means 'expectations'?

For me, it has done in the past. I've felt that I just wanted to leave, to walk for miles to clear my head before having to re-enter a place where I was shaped by my family's expectations. I did walk for miles sometimes, enjoying the fresh air; outdoors, I didn't have to act in a certain way to be 'accepted' by the world around me. Rather, I had space to think and just be—a freedom I didn't feel at home.

Do you sometimes find that home isn't a place where you can be yourself? Maybe it's just part of growing up, but I would suggest that we all face times when we feel a lot of pressure coming from our family members, despite knowing that love underlies our relationships. This means that being with family can be difficult, as we listen to the voice of each member and try to do as they ask, in order to be what we perceive as 'good enough' for them. It feels as if the weight of the world is on our shoulders as we try to live in a way that's pleasing to the rest of our family, denying ourselves space to breathe.

Where does all this 'shoulder weight' come from? Why do we feel we have to get everything right to gain our family's approval?

When I was thinking about these questions, I came to realise that sibling rivalry can be the origin of pressure and expectations. I have one sister, who is three years younger than me, and we share lots of time together, enjoying each other's company. We go to the same school, so, when my sister started Year Seven, some of her teachers knew me. This meant that they sometimes called my sister by *my* name, and seemed to expect her to get similar grades to mine. My sister felt pressure to equal or better my school performance, overshadowed by what I had done. These expectations frustrated her; having an older sibling at school seems to mean that you have to achieve a pre-set standard so that you're considered good enough by your teachers.

So perhaps family expectations can come from siblings. You feel you have to be as good as them in appearance, school grades and achievements. This competitiveness can pile on a huge amount of pressure, and perhaps that's where some of the 'shoulder weight' comes from.

A second source of pressure may be the belief that you have to 'fix' family arguments and make everything all right again. I used to think this a lot when I was little. I remember once trying to persuade my parents to stop arguing by apologising to them and promising to behave better for ever. I believed that I had caused their argument and that my 'sorry' and promises would end the conflict.

It didn't work, of course: the argument wasn't even about me. However, this didn't stop me from thinking that I had to get everything right, to make my family happy. Regardless of the real issues, I thought that if I fixed everything, I would be useful and good enough as a daughter.

This attitude followed me into my teenage years, contributing massively to the 'you're-not-good-enough' pressure that I felt was coming from my family. For about a year, between school Years Ten and Eleven, I felt under pressure in all areas of life, especially at home. Do you remember the 'masks' that I talked about in Chapter 3? In this particularly pressurised year, masks became my best friends. They greeted me each morning with the promise of hiding my imperfections and making me appear good enough, and then they abandoned me to tears and confusion each night.

Through no fault of my parents, I was convinced that I was not good enough for them. I believed I had to go through each day pretending that I had everything together and sorted. I held myself to perfection's standard, believing that if my parents saw my mistakes and struggles, they would be disappointed and I would have let them down. I had to be good enough on the outside so that they wouldn't discover my brokenness inside.

In this way, I built up a wall, my masks becoming defences for my heart. I distanced myself from everyone and tried to live a perfect life.

It all came to a head during a conversation with my dad, in the kitchen. It was a grey day and the light wasn't on, so we were conversing in grey gloom. Retrospectively, it was a perfect real-life example of the pathetic fallacy! I can't remember why we were there or what started the conversation, but we were there, and I was hurting. I was trying so hard to hold myself together and keep the tears locked inside. Then my dad said, 'Hannah, it looks like you've got the whole world on your shoulders...'

'It feels like it,' I replied, the tears irretrievable as they streamed down my face. My throat was burning, and I can't remember what happened next. Knowing me, I probably walked out and sat in my room, crying unseen. At any rate, I felt that I couldn't share my feelings or struggles with my dad. I thought that if I did, it'd be too embarrassing and painful for me to bear, and that he'd think less of me.

It's tough when it feels as if the person you are inside is not good enough for your family. It's difficult to take off the masks when you believe that your parents' expectations must be fulfilled in order for them to like you. It's hard, exhausting and soul-destroying, even more so when the pressure builds up between you and your family as a result of your hidden struggles.

On a related note, *Chicken Run* is one of my favourite films. (Seriously.) You know the part where Rocky throws a carrot into the gravy squirter inside the pie machine? And then the pressure builds up and up? The pressure climbs so high that eventually the whole machine explodes, destroying the building it's in and coating Mrs Tweedy in gross sticky gravy. It's an epic moment of cinematic justice: the chickens escape to their paradise, and the evil chicken farmers get covered in gravy. Anyway, I love it.

We can often become a bit like the gravy squirter. When we stop ourselves from sharing who we really are because we feel as if we're less than enough, the tension can build up between ourselves and our families. The pressure can build up so much that something gives way and we just explode. We find vent for our frustrations and our confusion somewhere, and, although our surroundings don't get soaked in gravy, these moments can have a destructive impact on our relationships.

Feeling pressure from family is a normal thing. As human beings, we all place expectations on each other. However, it can get really difficult when you feel you have to hide from the people closest to you, performing to what you perceive to be their standard. Keep reading, and together we'll uncover a new way to live.

The close-up

By now, you'll be used to these story-sections of each chapter, and I hope you find them useful. Here are a couple more, based on the family pressures we have been discussing. Which do you identify with? Why? Perhaps you could spend some time thinking about or writing down *your* story.

Joanna's an amazing girl. She has a hard-working, top-grade-achieving, good-looking, life-totally-sorted attitude, known by all her friends and noticed by all her year group. Even since primary school she's been marked for success, her achievements stacking up from a young age. And this is the year of applying to university: will an offer from a high-flying university be the next jewel in her crown?

It's not that she boasts about her achievements—she really doesn't. She's just good at what she does, and it'll be amazing to see what she does with her life.

So, applications are sent off and interviews attended across the year group, for a huge variety of courses at an overwhelming number of universities. The days of awaiting decision emails and letters from universities have arrived. Facebook buzzes with tension as some statuses just say, 'Waiting...', while others jubilantly announce, 'I've done it!' We all celebrate and congratulate; it is fantastic to see people achieving their dreams and reaching their top-choice universities.

Has *she*, though? Her timeline is silent; she's posted no news for weeks.

Then, the next day in school, news spreads like wildfire about who has achieved what offers for which universities. And our girl? She's done it too! A fantastic offer from her first choice, an amazing university with the toughest application process.

As is typical with school, rumours are hot on the heels of news. Apparently, she didn't really want the place. Why, then, did she apply? It seems that the expectations of her parents pushed her to push herself, to prove herself by aiming for the moon and catching all the stars in the process.

How does she feel? What is it like not to be able to choose where you go to uni, sacrificing your own choice for a tougher road mapped out by familial expectations? Our girl will probably accept her offer from that stunning university, but she'll feel the pressure, the strain, of hiding her true dreams so that her parents' expectations can be fulfilled.

Sophie lets her head rest against the back of the seat, closing her eyes as the train begins to pull slowly out of the station. The rhythm of the wheels gets faster and faster, the station and her home melting away behind her as university gets closer. She thinks about what she is going back to—the busy bustle of the city in summer, the relaxation of living with fellow students, the invigorating brainwork of studying. She looks forward to it, relishing already the freedom of being in control of what she does with her days. It's not like that at home, with family around.

Although they love her, her family often ask too much of her, entirely unaware of what they are doing. This is one of her worries about going back to uni: without her there as peacemaker, will her parents and siblings argue more?

The anxiety weighs on the young student's shoulders as she zips away on the train. She's the secret-keeper of the family, the one who glues the others together. There's an expectation that she'll defuse the arguments, mediate the conversations, fix the problems. She loves them, but can't her family see that this is all too much? She has a degree to work for, student house rent to pay, her own identity to find.

So, as the train track stretches ahead and home-life melts away, the expectations remain frozen in her mind, always there.

What God says

Earlier, we left 15-year-old me with tears streaming down my face in the corner of my bedroom, the world's weight sitting oppressively across my shoulders. Three years later,

I'm sitting in the same room, writing these words to you, sharing my stories and hoping you'll see that the whole world doesn't rest on your shoulders. I'm no longer crying in frustration and hiding behind numerous masks; I share most things with my parents and don't feel the weight of expectations bearing down on me so much, even though I still struggle. What happened to bring about such a change?

In short, God happened. In long… well, that could take a while. There are three things in particular that I want to look at with you, three things that God whispered into my ears and I heard. I hope they will help you in some way, when you're struggling with family pressures and difficult times.

The first thing happened in the summer of my Year Ten. Apart from the glorious sunshine and amazing free time, that particular summer—I can see now—was a gift wrapped in a struggle. Only a few months previously, I had started dating a wonderful boy, and adjusting to this new relationship was perhaps what caused some of the pressure and friction between my parents and me, and between who I was and who I was trying to be. Reading through some of my prayer journals from that time, I can see the struggle I was going through: 'God, help me to get rid of these negative feelings, especially towards my parents…'; 'I won't be perfect and it's ridiculous to feel so negative about failing…'; 'I'm just so frustrated…' I didn't feel as if I was good enough.

Among these prayers of struggle, however, there are glimpses of the hope that God brings. In particular, there are notes from when I read the book of Hosea, a beautiful book in the Old Testament which is essentially a 14-chapter-long account of God's great anger and his even greater love. The book opens with an acted-out metaphor, as God calls Hosea (the prophet-author of the book) to marry Gomer, a wife who is then unfaithful. Hosea represents God, and Gomer symbolises God's people, who were unfaithful to him: they turned away from him by worshipping false idols and forgetting the one true God. Instead of separating from Gomer completely, Hosea, as instructed by God, takes her home and loves her.

God is showing that he does the same for his people. To Hosea he says, 'Love her as the Lord loves the Israelites, though they turn to other gods' (3:1). This great love of God is seen again after several chapters of his wrath, as we read these startling words: 'How can I give you up…? How can I hand you over, Israel?… My heart is changed within me; all my compassion is aroused' (11:8). These are mind-blowing words, telling of God's deep love. Do you feel it? After sin and guilt and brokenness and God's great anger, he still can't bear to give his people—including you—up.

It goes even further than this. God makes promises to his people: 'I will heal their waywardness and love them freely, for my anger has turned away from them. I will be like the dew to Israel; he will blossom like a lily. Like a cedar of Lebanon he will send down his roots; his young shoots will grow' (14:4–6). God's outpouring of love continues.

All of this love hit the 15-year-old me powerfully. It was less of a whisper and more of a roar. There was this great love being offered to me, despite all the times I'd failed and all the times I'd put on masks to hide my vulnerability. I suddenly understood that God saw beyond my masks and into my brokenness, and in that brokenness he was calling me 'Loved daughter'. Even though I wasn't perfect, God proclaimed me worthy of his love.

That is the first discovery I want to share with you, and here is the second: because of this great love of God's, we can trust him on the inside, and so have confidence on the outside. Again, this ties into our discussion about image and real beauty in Chapter 3, but here we can see how it also applies to our family conflicts.

Do you remember, right back in the first chapter of this book, I mentioned my youth leader, Amy? There was one time when she shared a verse with me while we were enjoying cake and chat in Costa. The verse was Romans 15:13: 'May the God of hope fill you with all joy and peace as you trust in him, so that you may overflow with hope by the power of the Holy Spirit.'

This verse expresses the relationship between God's grace and our trust, showing that, as we trust God on the inside, he will fill us to overflowing with hope and joy and peace. As his love seeps into the depths of your heart, he will strengthen you on the inside so that you are confident on the outside.

To explain this further, I'm going to describe a picture that someone once shared with me. As we spoke, this person took my pen and my prayer journal and drew a picture of a teacup, sitting on a saucer, sitting on a plate. Then she drew a jug pouring water into the teacup. As the teacup filled up, she explained, the water would spill out on to the saucer, and then the plate.

Metaphorically speaking, I was the teacup in the picture. The saucer represented the people closest to me—family and friends—and the plate was an emblem of the wider world. The jug pouring water symbolised God. Do you see? It means that, as we let go of the things that hold us back and trust God to fill the emptiness left behind, he fills us with the water of his grace. As God continues this inpouring, that grace-water overflows first into our relationships with family and friends (the saucer), and then into the wider world (the plate). Trusting God allows his grace to transform us inside, and this transformation has a domino-like effect on the whole world. Although we sin and fall short of God's perfect standard, even though we're not good enough to receive his holiness, God restores us and rebuilds us by his grace so that we become more 'good enough' each day.

So far in this chapter, I have compared us to gravy squirters and teacups. Whatever next?! But how does the teacup picture help us with the issue of family pressure?

I would suggest that a deep trust in God's great love will allow us to have the confidence to take off our masks and be real with our parents and our families. Maybe our confidence will allow us to share our fears and struggles with them, letting them see beyond our defences and into our brokenness, so that they can help us not to feel so pressurised. Open and honest communication is a great way to solve problems, and God gives us the confidence we need to share and be vulnerable, especially when we feel scared of disappointing or failing those we love.

Then, more often than not, when we take off the masks, we realise that our families love us to pieces. Any dis-appointment or anger they may feel over the mistakes we make is overtaken by love—strong, powerful love that binds them to us. They want to see us safe and protected and held close. Ann Voskamp wrote a post for her blog, *A holy experience*, which reads like a letter to her daughters, explaining how her love for them means that she has to sometimes say 'No' when they ask to do particular things or go to particular places.

As daughters, we could read our families' or parents' 'No' as pressure, as expectation, as rules to live a life by—or we could read it as love. The words Voskamp writes are these:

'Look, I could tell you that you could go... but I love you too much.'[13] Your family's expectations may sometimes be straightforward ones that you have to talk through with the people involved, or they may be expressions of a love that is so strong that it actually hurts your parents to refuse your requests.

Even more than this, your parents' love for you means that they do see you as good enough. They do already accept you and hold you in their hearts as their loved and beautiful daughter. Think about the good times you've had with your family—all the times when your parents and siblings have brought out the best in who you are. In much the same way as God does, your family members love you and bring out your true character and personality, if you let them. They build you up, encourage you and help you to become the person God's created you to be. They champion you and love to see you be the best you can be, joyful and content and your own beautiful self.

A story I read in Jennifer Dukes Lee's book *Love Idol* captures this idea perfectly. She describes a race in which she and her daughter were running. Her own dad was calling out the names of all of the runners, even the last ones, as they crossed the finishing line. This is what she writes of her experience:

Then I heard my father's words for me: 'And that's my daughter, Jennifer!'

And I suppose the crowd was applauding me too. I can't be sure. All I remember are the words my father saved just for me, his daughter. I remember the welcome of a father who loves me and was waiting for me, a father who was pleased with me despite my performance.[14]

Lee heard the unconditional love of her father shouting from the finishing line, and she was encouraged, strengthened and built up by this love. Families really can be a blessing, and so, when we allow them to see the struggle and the (often self-inflicted) pressure and expectations upon us, we allow them to encourage us in love and bring out our best selves.

Perhaps my words aren't translating into your home or family situation at all. Perhaps it's completely different for you: you may come from a more difficult and less love-filled background. May I offer some hope to you? There is one thing that we can all hold on to, regardless of our family situations: God is, and for ever will be, our Father who loves us *so much*.

This is my third point, and I guess you could see it as a reiteration of my first. God's love is so big, however, that it's worth talking about again, and this time I want to talk specifically about God's love as our Father.

Are you familiar with the parable of the prodigal son (Luke 15:11–32)? It's a story that Jesus told, showing us the great grace and love of God. In the parable, we see a son abusing his father's love, taking his inheritance early and spending it on a luxurious, wasteful life in a faraway country. The son eventually spends all of his money so that he ends up living in desperate poverty. He's in the worst possible position, and just wants to return to his father and ask for forgiveness, hoping for a servant's position in his father's household at best. To return as a son will be impossible.

But how can he go back now? His father will never accept him, even as a servant: the father probably wants never to see him again. The son feels that he has exhausted his father's love because of the life that he has lived.

Eventually, the son makes up his mind to begin the

journey home, one dusty step at a time. He progresses slowly, reluctantly. Will his guilt ever leave him? Will his father show him mercy? Maybe he should just turn back and not even attempt to ask for that impossible forgiveness?

His questions melt away as he approaches his father's house. Out of fear? No—out of an overwhelming sense of being loved, as he sees his father running towards him, sprinting towards the son who thought he'd never be loved again. He's held in a hug, in the arms of the great loving grace of a father who's just so excited to see his son back home: 'He was dead and now he is alive, he was lost and now is found!' (see v. 24). This father is crazy about his son, fit to burst with excitement and joy. He loves him, and this love drowns out all the son's past mistakes. Failure simply falls away into the background, forgotten, as the father and son celebrate and feast on the best food they have.

This is how God feels about you. He seriously loves you this much. Picture yourself in the place of the prodigal son. Take those dusty steps towards God, and, as you walk, realise that God's tidal wave of love drowns out failure and mistakes, washing you clean and placing you at his table for the meal of a lifetime. You're God's *Loved Daughter*.

Love this amazing and free seems too good to be true, right? Surely there's a catch? Surely you have to earn this love? It can't really and truly be completely free? But just look at the prodigal son. He didn't do anything to earn his father's love; he just took steps to return home and opened his broken heart up to forgiveness. Do you see? This love is a free gift, a gift of astronomical grace. All God asks is that you come to him, being honest about who you are.

Philip Yancey puts it like this: 'Throughout the Bible, in fact, God shows a marked preference for "real" people over "good" people.'[15] God doesn't ask that you toe the line and reach a standard of 'good enough'. He doesn't ask for achievements and he doesn't require that you keep all the rules. God is a Father who loves your 'real' self, who longs for you to trust him with your messy heart and your tired brokenness. He takes that messy heart and transforms it into his image, grace shaping you into the beautiful daughter he created you to be. He's a Father who loves you back to life.

Let's end this section with some words from 2 Corinthians 6:18. Here, Paul reminds us of one of God's great promises: 'I will be a Father to you, and you will be my sons and daughters.' Even if you're feeling pressure from your family and you're struggling to take off your masks, God will always, *always*, be your Father.

Headphones time

We're here, again. I think you're probably used to encountering some questions about now, wrapping up the chapter and giving you space to think. It's good to get into a regular rhythm like this, isn't it? Find a quiet, undistracted place and breathe. Listen. Let go and find God.

- Do you sometimes feel as if you're not good enough for your family? Why?
- What expectations do you feel there are? What, in the actions of your family members, suggests that they expect these things of you?
- Choose one word to describe God's love. Why did you choose that word?
- How can you give God space to fill you to overflowing with the water of grace? How can you let your family encourage you and build you up, too?

- In your everyday living, do you try to be 'real' or to be 'good'? Why?

Soundtrack

'How deep the Father's love for us', by Stuart Townend, covered by Owl City.

As you listen, dwell in the great Father-love of God. What does it mean to be loved by God? Pray that God will build up trust and confidence in you, so that, where necessary, your family relationships can be restored and God's love seen over all.

6

Christian enough:
finding your feet in church

All other religions centre on people's righteousness—what we
do and how good we are. Real Christianity centres on Jesus'
righteousness—what he has done and how good he is.

JEFFERSON BETHKE[16]

The big picture

Curling my toes around pebbles, I look out across ocean
depths and wonder, 'Is this the edge of the world?' The
sound of the waves untangles me, slowing my heart to their
constant, steady rhythm. Breathe out worry, girl. You can
relax, hands in pockets and hair blown curly by salt air. What
anxiety could grip your heart in this beautiful place?

I'm standing on the outer edge of a stony beach at a coastal
village called Selsey. Separated from the beach by a ribbon of
road is the house I'm staying at, with my godmother and
some family friends.

One summer evening, after filling up on fajitas and fruit,
my sister and our two friends and I run across to the shore.
The air is infused with the colours of sunset as we paddle in
the bone-chilling shallows of the sea, until it gets too cold to
bear. We look for interesting stones; the best are the big ones,
wannabe boulders sticking out from dunes of small, smooth,

round pebbles. We haul our favourites together and build towers, fitting stones together to build strong structures. They won't be there by morning—the waves will dismantle them under the moonlight—but never mind. We'll build more towers tomorrow.

The Bible speaks of stones—'living stones' that 'are being built into a spiritual house'. I'd guess that this structure will be more sturdy than our Selsey beach-towers, built as it is on the 'cornerstone' that is Jesus Christ. Take a moment to read 1 Peter 2:4–10.

Read it? OK, let's explore. This passage shows us how the world works—who Jesus is, where we fit as Christians, and what happens to those who don't follow Christ. Peter gives us an overview of our identity as Christians together and the answer to the question 'What is church?'

I don't know what your experience of church is. Do you go often? Is church your second home, or is it the last place you'd want to find yourself? Whatever church is to you, Peter is giving you a picture of God's intention for his people.

Verses 4–6 introduce the image of 'living stones'. Read them again: what does Peter say about Jesus in these verses? What does he say about us as Christians?

Firstly, Peter calls Jesus 'the living Stone'. He quotes Isaiah 28:16, invoking the symbol of 'a chosen and precious cornerstone'. The cornerstone of a building is the first stone or brick; without it, there would be no foundation and the building would fall apart. On Selsey beach we knew that the first stone was important: we chose the biggest, flattest stone to be our tower's base.

Thus Peter declares that Jesus is the foundation. So what is Jesus the foundation for? Well, that's where we come in. Jesus is the cornerstone for us, the 'living stones' who 'trust in him' and are therefore 'being built into a spiritual house'.

Together, we are the walls and floor and ceiling of the 'spiritual house' that Jesus inhabits. We're the earthly representatives of God; we're the place where he dwells, the place from which he works. We're a place of safety and grace because we are built on Jesus, the cornerstone; we are like stones forming a shelter, a building, a beach-tower.

Therefore, we are church. If the stereotypical image of a church is a magnificent building with a spire and stained-glass windows, we are the spiritual equivalent. We are collectively God's house, with doors open to those who need to receive God's healing, grace and love.

Peter goes on, in verses 9 and 10, to describe our identity together. We are 'a chosen people': just as my friends and I chose stones on the beach, God chooses people to be his church. Peter then states that we are 'a royal priesthood'! Well, I don't know about you, but I am neither a priest nor related to the monarchy. To clarify, what Peter means is that we are called to be God's 'witnesses... to the ends of the earth' (Acts 1:8). We are chosen to give testimony to God's grace and power; this is what Peter means here by priestly work.

Peter goes on to call us 'a holy nation' and 'God's special possession'. As church, we are chosen, holy and special to God, and we are meant to be his representatives. We are chosen 'that [we] may declare the praises of him who called [us] out of darkness into his wonderful light'. We have a together-identity as oases of grace to the world, just as God is an ocean of grace to us.

This together-identity is a reflection of the Israelites' God-given identity, which was declared to them just before God gave Moses the ten commandments: 'Now if you obey me fully and keep my covenant, then out of all nations you will be my treasured possession. Although the whole earth is mine, you will be for me a kingdom of priests and a holy nation' (Exodus 19:5–6).

Do you see the similarities? The Israelites were God's first 'treasured possession', 'kingdom of priests' and 'holy nation'. The difference is in the way we *come into* our identity. For the Israelites, it was through obedience to the law. For us, it is through trust in Jesus. The Old Testament law showed that people could never adhere to God's holy standard: they needed a sacrifice to atone for sin, a saviour to lift them from death. This sacrifice and saviour we know to be Jesus, so our together-identity is a gift made possible by Jesus. This is how church should be, how God originally intended his people to live in community.

Despite this ideal picture, do you sometimes feel out of place in church? Are you the awkward stone that doesn't quite fit into the walls of the spiritual house, as if your edges were too jagged or your shape too small? When we built beach-towers, we made sure that the stones fitted together well, showing as few gaps as possible. If a stone didn't fit, we threw it away. Do you sometimes feel as if church has discarded you, telling you you're not good enough to be a part of the 'God gang'?

You're not alone. I think the occasional dysfunctionality of church is a symptom of our brokenness, our sin, life in a fallen world. Living stones can rub each other up the wrong way, grinding each other down to sand. Sometimes this rubbing action is good: as Christians, we should 'teach and admonish one another' (Colossians 3:16), helping each other's edges to become smooth, gentle and godly. If we teach and admonish by *shaming* each other, however—by saying 'You're not good enough' and demanding better behaviour—

the grinding work of the stones becomes unhealthy and we forget that 'the one who trusts in him will never be put to shame' (1 Peter 2:6).

Let me introduce you to Shame. You've already met him, but you may not know his name. He slithers unnoticed through our lives and our churches. He's like a snaky, slimy seaweed, growing chokingly on the living stones of the church, making us lose grip on each other and fall out of the walls of God's spiritual house.

His slime is in his words: 'You're not good enough.' Libby Vincent describes shame as 'the intensely painful feeling or experience of believing that we are flawed and therefore unworthy of love or belonging'.[17] Shame weakens us and holds us down by labelling us with failure: 'You were never good enough to belong, and you never will be. How dare you think that someone as sinful and imperfect as you would ever be good enough to be loved?'

Shame hurts; it makes us cover up. We've seen this in previous chapters, where we've discussed times when we feel we have to live in a particular way to be loved. Doesn't shame's hissing sound much like the hissing of our wall-mirrors, our exam grades, ourselves? Shame makes us put masks on to hide pain, even in church. It's no surprise that shame has always made people cover up: look at Adam and Eve, who 'made coverings for themselves' and 'hid from the Lord God' after they had disobeyed God by eating the forbidden fruit (Genesis 3:7–8).

But it's not just *after* we have sinned that we feel shame. We know that from the previous chapters too: often, it's shame that causes sin. It makes us forget the trustworthiness of God's love, persuading us to try to be perfect through our own strength.

Dr Kelly Flanagan, in his blog *UnTangled*, writes, 'Shame is the belief that what is inside of us is not good enough', leading to 'the search for something outside of us that will finally make us feel worthy'.[18] This search often leads us away from God to things we can immediately grasp, thinking that they will give us love and worth. Look again at Adam and Eve in Eden: read Genesis 3:1–8.

The snake hissed to Eve that God didn't want her to eat the fruit, 'for God knows that when you eat from it your eyes will be opened, and you will be like God' (v. 5). In other words, Satan labelled Eve as not good enough to be like God, and not worthy even to be with him. He shamed her, placing insecurity in her heart and causing her to doubt God's goodness. Thus she turned from God and ate the fruit, believing it would give her worth and make her good enough. She stopped relying on God's love and found herself guilty, cast out of Eden.

We all do this. Slippery shame makes us lose our grip on Jesus, the cornerstone, leading us to insecurity and often to sin. You'd expect church, a place meant as a grace-full shelter, to be the last place you'd find this, right?

Wrong. Church can sometimes be rife with shame, making people feel that they're not good, worthy or holy enough to be loved either by the church community or by God. It's true, in a way: the Bible tells us that 'all have sinned and fall short of the glory of God' (Romans 3:23). We all fail, falling short of God's standard of impossible perfection.

Despite this, we sometimes don't accept Jesus' grace. Instead, we try, in our own strength, to achieve perfection equal to God's. Jefferson Bethke equates this to trying to jump 2500 miles across the North Pacific Ocean: 'Trying to be good enough to earn heaven is like trying to jump to Hawaii from California. Everyone looks like an idiot, some drown, some get three feet, some get ten feet, but no one even gets close to Hawaii.'[19]

Can you see the traits of those of us who strive for heaven on our own merit? We're idiots and we don't even get close. Yet this doesn't stop us. Church culture may even promote the attitude that there are things we can do to be 'better Christians', to become people more worthy of God's love. If we don't do those things, we can feel as if we don't belong, as if we're so far away from Hawaii that we will never get there.

Maybe you think of church's expectations in terms of the 'don'ts'. You believe that love and acceptance from God's people and God arise from following rules: if you don't drink, listen to unChristian music, gossip, lie or steal, you might receive God's love. Christianity is often presented as a checklist of rules, a standard you have to achieve in order to be worthy of God's love.

Conversely, you might feel unworthy of church life when you see other Christians 'doing life' so much better than you. They've got it all together, they never make mistakes and they always help others. They've been on mission trips, they've read the Bible cover-to-cover more than once, and, to top it all off, they're kind, bubbly and confident. They know exactly where their identity lies and are fully secure in God.

Bethke testifies, 'I decided to copy what "being a Christian" was all about by watching others... I thought that if I did enough Christian things, it would bring peace to my life. It didn't work.'[20] It's true that we should learn from each other, like stones rubbing each other down to smoothness, but we can't copy each other. It's got to be our own journey, supported by others but not copied from them, learning from the inside out who God wants us to be. Trying to live outside in, by adopting external behaviour in the hope that it will change our hearts, is pointless. The heart's got to change first, and that's not something you can copy from anyone.

Most of the time, church doesn't purposely present these expectations. Stones don't choose to have seaweed growing on them. If I were a stone, I'd want to be smooth, clean and seaweed-free, but that doesn't stop seaweed from being there. In the same way, church's good intentions don't always prevent shame from having an effect.

I'll return to this question: are you the awkward stone that doesn't seem to fit? Read on, and together we'll uncover how you can find your feet in church. If you're not an awkward stone and love your church, that's great! Would you like to read on too? Wear someone else's shoes, and learn how you can help to include and encourage people in church, making them feel less awkward and more loved.

The close-up

I've only included one story this time. Pause, read and reflect: how is this story similar to or different from your experiences of church?

The church youth leader picked up the colourful magazines lying on the coffee table. Their headlines declared the latest celebrity news: 'Jessica suffers fake tan fail!';[21] 'Duchess Kate to visit Downton Abbey set';[22] 'Kim Kardashian "goes blonde".'[23]

After a few moments, the youth leader asked the girls around her, 'So, who actually reads this rubbish?' Most of the girls immediately shook their heads—of course they didn't! Why would they, such good Christian girls, read such bad, gossipy, unChristian magazines? They had resisted the temptation and were *obviously* more holy for doing so.

Bethany, sitting in one of the armchairs, looked around, blushed and slowly raised her hand. The rest of the girls looked round at her with a mixture of judgement and pity. Bethany explained, feeling the need to justify herself: 'I only read them on holiday with my mum. It's just something to do when we're relaxing and it's raining.'

The others listened quietly, awkwardly, not knowing quite what to say to a girl who read the wrong type of magazines. Moving on, the youth leader asked another question: 'Has anyone seen *Bridget Jones' Diary*?'

Bethany was alone in raising her hand for the second time. The others were far too good to watch a 15-rated movie in which some people swear and a couple make love. Their minds hadn't been corrupted by viewing such things. They looked over at Bethany with the same awkward mixture of pity and condemnation. They couldn't reconcile watching this film with being a Christian; it just shouldn't be done!

Bethany shrank back into her armchair, avoiding eye contact with anyone else. She felt odd, different, isolated. Even worse, the judgement and condemnation she felt directed towards her for reading gossip magazines and watching that movie made her feel terrible. One sentence repeated in her mind: 'I'm a bad Christian.'

Bethany decided that she should clean up her act before coming to youth group again. She would stop reading gossip magazines and watching unacceptable films, and somehow make herself more holy, more Christian. Then she'd be accepted into the youth group, eventually counted as one of their own. Maybe God would want something to do with her then, too.

What God says

When Jesus walked on earth, there was a group of people who presented their lives as perfect, holy and righteous. They didn't pay attention to their hearts, to who they were inside. They expected others to copy their behaviour, or be judged. These people were called Pharisees.

Once, Jesus was dining at a Pharisee's house. (You can read about it in Luke 11:37–42.) Quickly, the conversation turned to deep matters and uncomfortable questions, sparked by the fact that Jesus didn't wash before he sat down to eat. If the Pharisees were shocked at that, imagine how shocked they were when Jesus started accusing them: 'You Pharisees clean the outside of the cup and dish, but inside you are full of greed and wickedness. You foolish people! Did not the one who made the outside make the inside also?' (vv. 39–40).

The Pharisees had forgotten that God sees not only the outside but the inside as well. They had magnified God's laws so that all they cared about was external behaviour. Putting on a good show, regardless of their heart, was their talent.

Jesus showed them that relationship with God was not about performance or about being 'righteous' by adhering to rules. He wanted to go further than skin-deep, illustrating the idea with a practical example. He described the Pharisees' tithing, explaining how they'd missed the point completely: 'You neglect justice and the love of God' (v. 42). Tithing was meant to be an expression of love to God and a means of bringing about justice, but the Pharisees used it as an action with which to earn God's favour. Jesus raised the standard, saying that relationship with God stems from the heart: no amount of righteous actions will make us right with God if our heart doesn't beat for him first.

This passage was a bit of a wake-up call for me when I first read it. I realised I had been putting on a performance as a 'good Christian girl', self-righteously doing what God asked while judging those who made mistakes. The whole time, my heart was hurting, broken and crying for something to change. The change came when I realised that Jesus wants my whole self, not just my actions. He wants my heart to beat for him, not just my hands to perform his will dutifully.

It's like smiling. Some people smile only with their lips, their eyes staying cold or proud or sad. Jesus wants us to smile with our eyes as well as our lips. He wants our heart to be in our actions.

Smiling with our eyes is a challenge. It means we have to take off our masks and be vulnerable, and that can hurt. I hid behind the rules of a good Christian life because I thought that's what mattered, and I thought that's what would make people in church like me. They couldn't possibly like the mess I was inside, could they? I was too scared to be myself.

But that's what Jesus came to fix. Jesus came to free our hearts from fearful insecurity and teach us how to live freely, letting our eyes smile and our hearts beat loud through our actions. He came to transform you from the inside out. John 1:12 says this: 'But whoever did want him, who believed he was who he claimed and would do what he said, he made to be their true selves, their child-of-God selves' (*THE MESSAGE*). Jesus came to transform you into your true, beautiful self.

The first thing you need to remember is that we are all broken inside. We all fall short of God's glory, and, at some point, we've all had to face the fear of being ourselves, by taking off our masks. You're not the only person who struggles with fitting in at church; there is no such thing as a perfect person.

This is what makes our together-identity, as church, amazing. It's an identity given to us not because we deserve it but because God chooses and uses imperfect people to build his kingdom. God uses the unexpected, the weak, the downtrodden and the lonely to represent him.

In the introduction to his book *Dysciples*, Krish Kandiah writes, 'I have coined the term "dysciples" to describe those of us who feel dysfunctional in our following of Jesus, whether that is because we find discipleship beyond us or beneath us, too hard or too easy, unnerving or unnatural.'[24] We are all 'dysciples' or 'awkward stones' in one way or another. The good news is that God uses dysfunctional and awkward people to achieve his purposes—people like Moses.

Moses was an unlikely choice as a leader of God's people. He was from an oppressed people, the Hebrews, and he was a murderer and a man who fled in fear. Yet God breathed a new purpose into Moses' life—to deliver the Hebrews from under the Egyptians' oppression. Moses knew his weaknesses and was afraid. He was ashamed; he didn't feel good enough to be God's mouthpiece, asking, 'Since I speak with faltering lips, why would Pharaoh listen to me?' (Exodus 6:30).

We can often feel like Moses, ashamed of our weaknesses, and scared to let our hearts and our hands carry out God's plans. We sometimes don't feel good enough to be a stone in the walls of God's spiritual house. But hear this: Moses freed thousands of people from the Egyptians.

God used imperfect Moses and made him strong. 2 Corinthians 12:9 records God's promise to Paul: 'My grace is sufficient for you, for my power is made perfect in weakness.' So even you, feeling that you're not Christian enough to be in church or holy enough to do good for God, will do great things when you trust God's power to be your strength.

God has wild, unimaginable dreams for you. Do you think that Moses expected to be remembered for thousands of years? God has plans for you: 'We are God's handiwork, created in Christ Jesus to do good works, which God prepared in advance for us to do' (Ephesians 2:10).

To take hold of this vision, we need to let go of masks and fear. Kelsey Kirkegaard, on the blog *A Girl Like Me*, imagines God's voice as she writes:

You can choose the safety of decisions that can be wrapped in your control, tied up neatly with a bow and leaving you with a small content little life or you can choose the great adventure of throwing your hands up and leaping into the unknown, listening to my still small voice urging you ahead, resulting in dreams and victories only possible when you give me your tiny fist of control and let me breathe life into dreams unimaginable.[25]

Stunning words, right? Elijah was faced with this choice as he lay down to die in the desert. Esther had to decide whether or not to use her beauty for God's purposes. Moses had to choose whether to go with God or stay in Midian when God appeared and spoke from the burning bush. It's a choice presented to each of us: stay where we're comfortable or follow God?

The latter is a great adventure, and it's scary. But God has given us all this gift, and, as each 'living stone' says 'Yes' to God, they will be placed in the wall of his spiritual house. When we embark on God's adventure, we stop comparing ourselves with other Christians. We shed the seaweed of shame from around us, as we realise that God wants us to live unashamed and free. We stop copying others and instead become our truest selves. This is how church is built, through an awakening to who we are.

Ephesians 2:19–22 emphasises the fact that when we accept God's great adventure we become 'a holy temple in the Lord... a dwelling in which God lives by his Spirit'. I love the words 'In him the whole building is joined together' (v. 21). To be 'in Jesus' means to grow in relationship with him and live according to his purposes. When we do this, we join together with other Christians, encouraging each other and fitting together as walls and floor and ceiling.

How can you take hold of God's adventure for you? Pray (we'll talk more about this in the next chapter). Grow where you're planted: take root in God wherever you find yourself. Let God work through you in the situations you are in at church. Let him give you peace on the inside that overflows to confidence on the outside, as you know that you are held firm on Jesus the cornerstone.

If you're already doing these things and have found your feet in church, why don't you look out for those who do feel like awkward stones? Pray with them and encourage them. Let them know that God wants to release them from fear into a new and beautiful life where their heart can beat freely. Listen to their dreams, struggles, pain, joys and worries. There's an organisation called Acorn Christian Healing Foundation that works to equip people in these sorts of listening skills; if you want to learn about how to help people who feel out of place and not good enough for church, you could look into some of the work they do. (You'll find details in the Resources section at the end of this book.)

As you walk into church, remember that your together-identity is to be a spiritual house for God. Hold on to the fact that you are a 'living stone' who is 'never put to shame', because of your trust in Jesus. Everyone in your church is broken somehow, yet is given a place in God's house. There's no such thing as 'Christian *enough*'; there are just broken people holding their hands out for grace.

Headphones time

Pause and reflect on all you've read, thought about and connected with in this chapter. Here are some questions to help you along the way.

- Think of a time when you felt ashamed or embarrassed. What three words would you use to describe that feeling? How did you respond to it?
- What do you feel you have to do in order to be a 'good Christian'? Reflect on each thing, in light of the fact that God gives you love and worth by grace alone.
- What do you dream of doing? What makes your heart come alive? Do you think that these things could be a part of your God-given adventure? Perhaps share these things with someone in your church.
- Read 1 Corinthians 12:12–30. How does this passage describe church?
- Find some stones. On each stone, write a word of Galatians 6:2—'Carry each other's burdens, and in this way you will fulfil the law of Christ'—reflecting on how we as church can carry each other's burdens. Give each stone to a person in your church, explaining what our together-identity is. This is something you could do with your youth group.

Soundtrack

'Cathedral made of people' by Downhere.

This song explores what it means to be God's 'spiritual house', living stones built by and for and through him. Which words of the song stand out to you?

7

Held enough:
rhythms for connecting with God

Come near to God and he will come near to you.

JAMES 4:8

If you had to choose either prayer or Bible reading to keep in your life, which would you choose? Think carefully: what are the pros and cons of each? Which is the more important?

This question was an icebreaker at an event I attended a couple of years ago. We sat in groups and discussed it for several minutes; I think I chose prayer. As the discussion ended, the speaker looked around the room, grinned and said, 'Trick question!' We all grinned back sheepishly. How had we fallen into the trap of seriously discussing such a ridiculous hypothetical situation?

It's a ridiculous situation because prayer and the Bible are equally essential tools for drawing close to God, to find out who he is and who we are. 'Tools' doesn't seem quite the right word; we are not dissecting God with prayer or trying to create a formula for knowing him by reading the Bible. Rather, in praying and reading God's word, we are talking to a person, getting to know him and letting him speak to us. Instead of using operating-table tools to cut God open, we're meeting over a coffee table, using time, conversation and honesty to get to know our Father. Perhaps a better word would be 'gifts': both prayer and the Bible are gifts given so that we can know God.

Even though I know the importance of prayer and the Bible, I sometimes abandon God-time to a perpetual tomorrow, in favour of some other thing today. How often, when choosing between God-time and books/friends/food/insert-distraction-of-your-choice-here, have you chosen God-time? If you are confident in saying, 'Oh, most of the time', that is fantastic. Keep it up, girl! You really are doing great.

But if, like me, you answer that question with a guilty sideways look and a slight blush, perhaps it's not so fantastic —and you know it. What are your excuses for forsaking time with the Creator of the universe?

For me, it's often because of my feelings. 'I just don't feel like praying right now.' I don't want to get up early to spend time learning to understand the Bible. I feel too tired. 'I don't have the energy.' I know God wants me even when I'm struggling, but I don't feel like telling him about it now. 'What if God challenges me? I don't feel as if I have the time to do something new.' Man, I'm just not feeling that holy vibe right now—maybe later?

Wake up! Seriously, open your eyes. Look at those excuses and then read this verse: 'Pray in the Spirit *on all occasions with all kinds of prayers and requests.*' That's Ephesians 6:18a (emphasis added). This is 1 Thessalonians 5:16–18: 'Rejoice always, *pray continually*, give thanks in all circumstances; *for this is God's will for you* in Christ Jesus' (emphasis added, again).

How do our excuses compare with that? Do you think that Paul, who wrote those words, would understand you if you said, 'I just don't feel like praying right now'? Paul was a man on fire for God, absolutely sold out for his Saviour. He would look at you strangely if you told him you weren't up to praying; to him, prayer was a privilege to be taken seriously and fully. Why would you pass up on an opportunity to talk to *God*?

We can't get away with feelings-based excuses. When we come to God, we need to realise that his truth has so much more authority than our emotions. His truth is unchanging and unfaltering, even when our feelings fluctuate and shift. 2 Timothy 2:13 says, 'If we are faithless, he remains faithful.' God always remains faithful to his people: remember Hosea's message? By contrast, our faithfulness and feelings are transient and fleeting. We need to listen primarily to God's truth instead of our emotions, as that's the rock that remains steadfast.

The words of C.S. Lewis capture the idea perfectly: 'If you look for truth you may find comfort in the end; if you look for comfort you will not get either comfort or truth, only... wishful thinking to begin, and in the end, despair.'[26] The pursuit (or non-pursuit) of truth affects our emotions; for Lewis, truth offers eventual comfort, and no truth offers only despair. C.J. Mahaney puts it like this: 'When we focus first on truth... feelings follow! And they'll be *reliable* feelings because they're anchored in truth.'[27]

So we should come to God in pursuit of who he is, not in pursuit of warm, fuzzy feelings. Although how we feel is important to God, we should rely on God's truth first. 'Steep yourself in God-reality, God-initiative, God-provisions. You'll find all your everyday human concerns will be met' (Luke 12:31, *THE MESSAGE*). Immerse yourself in God's truth first—feelings follow.

I wrote myself a note a year ago which speaks into this: 'The best way to start painting is to get your paint brushes out. If you don't want to write, get a pen to paper and write. If you don't feel like praying and lack the motivation, the best way to start praying is to pray.'

The best way to start praying is to pray. With that in mind, I have adopted a different structure for this chapter. I'm going to spend time discussing different rhythms that you may find useful for connecting with God. Some of these rhythms are for individual God-times; others may be good for groups. They are all adaptable, and none are obligatory; this isn't a spiritual checklist that you must work through. They are just ideas for how you could draw near to God.

Before we discuss these different rhythms, I would like to look at some of the truths we can use to counter negative, apathetic emotions when it comes to prayer. Firstly, God, not you, began this conversation. As Jesus breathed his last on the cross, the way was opened up for you to converse with the divine. Luke 23:45 says that, as Jesus died, 'the curtain of the temple was torn in two'. The temple curtain had, for centuries, separated God's people from God's presence— and now the curtain was being torn apart. God was made accessible by Jesus' curtain-rending death. Jesus is who he says he is: 'I am the way and the truth and the life. No one comes to the Father except through me' (John 14:6). You could never have torn that curtain, but the great news is that it has been torn for you.

This is the essence of prayer: it is a connection made possible entirely by God, the divine reaching out to the broken. We can never build ladders high enough or bridges long enough; we simply cannot reach God through our own strength. We must rely on God's promise to us that the way is open.

Reminding ourselves that God enables prayer is greatly

humbling. Humility is a response to the fact that time with God is a gift, given because we cannot get close to God through our own strength. In prayer, I know that I can drop the act, take off the masks and let him have my mess. I don't have to impress God in order to earn the gift of time with him. I don't have to be perfect in God's presence; instead, my heart can beat strong and secure, even when it's raw, because I know that a God who gave so much to talk with me cares about that rawness and will heal it.

Therefore, feeling 'not good enough' is not a reason to avoid God-time. God already knows that I'm not good enough for him. That makes relationship with him all the sweeter, because I know I am only there because of his grace, the grace of a God who sees past my brokenness right to the core of who I am. He sees the beauty humming at my centre, a beauty he placed there at creation, and he shows me how to get there. God restores me.

This restoration is a wild adventure. Running after God opens doors, eyes and hearts. God surprises us with what he brings out of relationship with him, so get ready to be challenged, excited, impassioned and made new as you open your heart to God, just as Elijah was when he stood outside his cave on the mountain.

Also, don't beat yourself up about not spending 100 per cent of your time in prayer. I know I've sometimes thought, 'I'm just not praying enough! What will God think of me?' We do need to make every effort to be with God, but it needs to be because of our desire and love, not duty and obligation. In *The Prayer Course*'s opening video, Pete Greig tells a story about his children. Greig had just finished writing a book, which meant he hadn't had much time to spend with his family. To celebrate, he took his wife and children to a restaurant with a playground outside, and Greig told his two sons to go and play. One of them ran off happily to enjoy the sunshine and swings straight away. The other paused, turned to his dad and said, 'Daddy, I've missed you.' He climbed into his father's lap and wouldn't leave.[28]

Greig related this moment to prayer. His two sons' different actions didn't make him love one more than the other. The second son didn't have to stay with his dad; it wouldn't have been wrong for him to go and play outside. But he *chose* to share his emotions, love and time with his dad, ministering to his dad's heart in the process. Prayer is the same: it doesn't make God love us more; it isn't wrong to go and enjoy the world that God's given us. It is a choice, and we minister to God's heart when we share our lives with him.

A final truth I want to underline is this: God wants *you*, honest *you*, coming just as you are. These words from Jeremiah 17:9–10 say it all: 'The heart is hopelessly dark and deceitful, a puzzle that no one can figure out. But I, God, search the heart and examine the mind. I get to the heart of the human. I get to the root of things. I treat them as they really are, not as they pretend to be' (*THE MESSAGE*). Pray honestly, therefore. Go into a quiet room with no distractions, and explore rhythms of prayer that you could adopt into your own life. Let your life become a worship song with God's heartbeat as its rhythm.

Rhythms

You don't have to spend God-time exactly as I've suggested below; there's no right way to pray. We have an infinitely creative God and we are made in his image. Be creative about how you share your heart with him.

How can you converse with God when you first wake up?

The clichéd reason for being in a grumpy mood is that you 'got out of bed on the wrong side'. There are many problems with this cliché, the greatest being: how can I get out of bed on the wrong side if my bed's next to the wall? It's these questions that keep me up at night.

Dietrich Bonhoeffer, a great theologian, shed light on this situation by writing, 'The morning prayer determines the day.'[29] Evidently it's not the side of the bed that determines your mood; rather, it's the attitude you choose to start your day with. Do you start with a prayerful few minutes of reflecting on God's truth, or do you immediately let your feelings colour your view of the day, inwardly complaining about all the stuff you'll have to deal with?

Whatever your answer, I think the former approach is the more favourable. Focusing on God's truth first thing sets you up for the rest of the day, reminding you of the grace that brought you here. There are many methods you could use to meet with God in the morning, one of which is called 'morning pages'.

Emily Freeman blogged about morning pages, quoting the author Julia Cameron on their definition. What it comes down to is a practice of writing three pages of stream-of-consciousness thought each morning. Freeman writes, 'If prayer is a deep breath in, the Morning Page is a cleansing breath out.'[30]

A cleansing breath out could be exactly what you need as you start the day. Writing down your worries, frustrations and thoughts clears out the cobwebs cluttering the corners of your mind and leaves your soul free to breathe in prayer.

Freeman calls her morning pages notebook her 'to-be' notebook, rather than a 'to-do' notebook; maybe you need to give yourself the space just to be and rest, before you do everything the day asks of you. After all, God made us as human beings, not human doings.

A second rhythm invites the Bible into your morning prayer. Have you ever used a book of devotional notes to help you pray? They usefully give you a Bible verse and reflection to start your day with. Alternatively, you could focus on one psalm or Bible passage a week, taking a verse or couple of verses each morning to dwell on, reflect on and pray about. With this rhythm, you're looking at the truth of God first and then responding in prayer, very much like a conversation. (Remember the coffee table I mentioned at the start of this chapter?) This conversation will continue through the day: when I've read the Bible in the morning, the verses I've reflected on seem to pop into my head whenever I need to be reminded of God's love.

A final morning rhythm I want to share with you is slightly more active. (Feel free to tone down the activity if you're not a morning person.) I have an exercise bike (sounding ominous already?) and each morning, I try to wake myself up with 20 minutes of cycling. So where does prayer come in? Well, as I cycle, I pray.

I pray 'thank you', 'please' and 'sorry' prayers, bringing my day and feelings to God. Once I've prayed for myself, I pray for my family, boyfriend and friends at school. I pray for the people I will encounter. I pray for you, because you're the person this book is for.

In other words, as I cycle, I find space to talk to God and to 'widen my circle of prayer'. This is an idea I heard recently at church. The concept is that you start with a small circle as you pray for yourself and your day, and then the circle widens as you pray for more and more people.

It's not the cycling that prompts these prayers. It's the rhythm of doing something regularly that reminds me to talk to God. Could you build prayerful regularity into your mornings? You could go for a run or go downstairs and curl up in your favourite armchair. You could pray while you shower. Whatever you do, a great way to converse with God as you wake up is to attach prayer time to a regular activity, letting it be a reminder for you to seek God.

How can you converse with God during the day?

Take a walk. I don't know what it is about being outside, but a good old romp across fields or a stroll around the block has a great untangling effect. Walking means hearing the tramp of shoes on the ground; breathing in beautiful fresh air; letting your hair be tangled and teased by the wind's fingers. (I used to imagine that the wind was God's fingers twisting and knotting and unknotting my hair, making me feel loved.) Even if you can't walk outside, just being outside brings great freedom. Your soul finds space to breathe in the open air.

Walking without a particular purpose prompts you to listen. You listen to yourself as your thoughts ramble and tumble over one another. You listen to the world, noticing what's around you—the bumpy texture of tree trunks, the pink of cherry blossom, the sky's colours of grey and gold, a grandma and grandson crossing the road, a feather caught on the pavement, the exquisite spring buds next to the last crinkly leaf of autumn, the sweet sound of birds descanting over all the other noises.

Anne Shirley, the heroine of L.M. Montgomery's deliciously good book *Anne of Green Gables*, asks this question:

Why must people kneel down and pray? If I really wanted to pray I'll tell you what I'd do. I'd go out into a great big field all alone, or into the deep, deep woods, and I'd look into the sky— up—up—up—into that lovely blue sky that looks as if there was no end to its blueness. And then I'd just feel *a prayer.'* [31]

Sometimes, words cannot contain the depth and wonder of a prayer. Anne had it right: there is something about being immersed in God's beautiful creation that makes talking to him easier. Why not take a long and wandering walk? Let that be your time of listening, breathing and communing with God.

Another way to listen is to be still and silent. We so rarely take time to be fully silent, especially now that smartphones and social media have placed the world unhelpfully at our fingertips. We refuse to let ourselves rest; we never taste the repose that grace gives.

Yet it's in the Bible: 'Be still, and know that I am God' (Psalm 46:10); 'The Lord will fight for you; you need only to be still' (Exodus 14:14). Jesus went away to lonely, quiet places to pray without distraction. Why don't you do the same? Soul-work happens in silence; Emily Freeman writes, 'Stillness is to the soul what decluttering is to the home.'[32] Does your soul feel cluttered? Go and find a still space.

When I was on Share Jesus International's FRESH leadership course a few years ago, I had an opportunity to be still. We were staying for the weekend at Cliff College, Derbyshire. From 7 to 8 o'clock on the Saturday morning, we spent an hour in silence. No phones or communication were allowed: this time was for us and God.

I hadn't realised it, but my soul needed that stillness. As I sat on the ground in front of a bench at the top of the sloping apple orchard, my soul untangled in the early morning mist. I had been in pain for weeks with stress-induced backache, and I really needed God, so he met me in my pain and taught me to breathe.

He told me to breathe out all of my worries, pains, insecurities... and breathe in his grace, love, forgiveness. He told me to pour out my heart to him and let him fill me with grace. (It sounds a bit like 'morning pages', doesn't it?) I sat there in silence, just breathing.

At the end of the hour I felt refreshed and strengthened by the groundwork God had done in my soul. Why don't you carve out some time for silence? Disconnect from everything else in order to connect with God.

Another rhythm involves journalling—using paper instead of silence as a space for listening to God. A blank notebook contains so many possibilities; a new notebook always gives me thrills, because I know that struggle and soul-work will happen between its pages.

Pick up a notebook and create space to collect thoughts, develop ideas, write out prayers and record God's words. My journals contain an assortment of prayer-sparking items— Bible verses, conversations, flowers, photos, drawings, newspaper articles and quotations from books or blogs. It's as if the notebook is an overspill of the thoughts and prayers in my heart.

If you do adopt journalling as a rhythm, remember that journals aren't the 'product' of time spent with God. Intimacy with God is not about productivity. Journals are simply a means to an end, something that helps a heart to become a canvas on which God can paint his words.

All of the rhythms we've talked about already can do pretty deep soul-work, but, as I said at the beginning of this chapter, it's not just about prayer. It's about the Bible too. Bible study can be a tough discipline. It's difficult to read and understand ancient texts that are steeped in history and a very different culture. C.J. Mahaney voices our reservations: 'After all, who wants to spend the mental energy it takes to think carefully and intensely about the Scriptures? Who has time to study? Who has time to meditate?'[33]

There is a hint of irony in his words. We should *desire* to create time to study God's word, not make excuses about why we can't. Like prayer, it's a privilege of vital importance. Paul writes, 'All scripture is God-breathed' (2 Timothy 3:16). Who wouldn't want a lungful of that?

So, what can you do to study the Bible? First, read it, paying close attention. Get to grips with what it means by using Bible notes and commentaries, which give you a wide range of information and interpretation. (Check out the Resources section at the end of this book for some Bible notes you could look at.) Ask a lot of questions too: dive deep down into the passage you're studying. Try to memorise scripture. You never know when you might need a reminder of who you are in God and how much he loves you.

Finally, find people with whom you can pray and study the Bible. We saw in the last chapter that the church is God's people, intentionally seeking God together. In Acts 1:14, we read of the early church that 'they all joined together constantly in prayer'. The church was built on a foundation of 'together prayer', of God's people unitedly communing with God. Moreover, the Bible was originally read in communal settings, to groups—so when it says 'you', it often means 'you *plural*, as a church' rather than 'you *individually*, as one person'. Studying the Bible in groups reveals new truths and helps us to know Jesus collectively. Talk to people in your church, youth group, family or Christian Union: who could you seek God with?

How can you converse with God just before you go to sleep?

The daily examen is a practice that helps you to reflect on the day you've just had and commit the next day to God. The 2015 Lent podcast series from 24–7 Prayer discusses this rhythm, splitting it into five actions:

- Make yourself aware of God's presence.
- Reflect thankfully on your day.
- Ask yourself, 'How did my day make me feel?'
- Choose one thing to pray for.
- Look ahead to tomorrow.

You can find the full series at www.24-7prayer.com/podcasts.

The examen could take five minutes or 50, but each time I have practised it, I have been amazed at how much depth comes out of intentionally processing my day. Jo Swinney, in her book *God Hunting*, concludes that the examen 'is a lot more productive than mulling over the day and dwelling on all the things you wish you'd done differently'.[34] Do you ever find yourself 'mulling' in this way? Maybe the examen could change your attitude from regretful mulling to grateful reflection on God's gifts scattered throughout your day.

Alternatively, you could choose not to sleep. I've already mentioned the 24–7 Prayer movement; true to its name, it's a movement that encourages people to pray 24 hours a day, seven days a week. One way in which they do this is by equipping people to set up 24–7 prayer rooms, rooms set aside especially for continual prayer. You may have had the privilege to visit or be a part of a prayer room before; if you haven't, get involved! Visit 24–7 Prayer's website (listed in the Resources section at the back of this book). Suggest that your church set up a prayer room. You could visit a prayer room (perhaps sign up for a 3.00 am shift). God can be known in every minute, so this could be a new and creative way for you to engage with God in prayer.

I hope this has been a useful chapter for you, giving you some ideas for spending time with God. I know there are many more, and I know that they can be explored in much more depth than I have discussed them here. I've tried to give you some starting points for connecting with God, for journeying with him on this pilgrimage called 'life'. I hope I've revealed to you that this is a relationship we're talking about. There's no formula for relationships, just many creative ways to love and be loved.

I will finish with this invitation from Jesus in Matthew's Gospel:

'Are you tired? Worn out? Burned out on religion? Come to me. Get away with me and you'll recover your life. I'll show you how to take a real rest. Walk with me and work with me—watch how I do it. Learn the unforced rhythms of grace. I won't lay anything heavy or ill-fitting on you. Keep company with me and you'll learn to live freely and lightly.' (Matthew 11:28–30, The Message)

This is a beautiful invitation to keep company with Jesus and 'learn the unforced rhythms of grace'. Jesus invites you into his presence because he loves you and wants to spend time with you. He wants to give you rest and grace and joy. You can lay down your attempts to earn love and acceptance, and instead find love in Jesus' arms. He holds you, enough for you to let go of everything else.

So, just do it. Go to Jesus; keep company with him. Let him teach you a new way of living life to the full. Pray, girl, all the time, with every step. Be honest: admit you've had enough of the try-hard life. Meet God over a coffee table; let your heart be held by him.

Headphones time

Think about what rhythms you could adopt to help you draw near to God, and maybe try a few. Otherwise, here are some pointers to help you shape your thinking about some of the things we have discussed.

- What holds you back from conversing with God? What struggles do you face when it comes to communicating with him?
- Voice the request of the disciples for yourself: 'Jesus, teach us to pray.' Go to Luke 11 to find Jesus' response.
- Watch the video 'Connecting with God' by Jennie Allen, at http://youtu.be/R-U8mk8IGTw. What stood out most for you?
- Read Hebrews 4:14–16. What does it mean to have Jesus as the 'great high priest'? How does this build on the truth that Jesus opened the way for us to be with God?
- Make an invitation from God to you, using Matthew 11:28–30. Keep it somewhere you will see it regularly, as a reminder that God loves it when you spend time with him.

Soundtrack

'To our God' by Bethel Music, from their album *Without Words*.

Prayer can be creative, spoken without words, yet with honesty and truth. What's your creative way of conversing with God?

8

Created enough

We've reached the end of our journey, a journey similar to Elijah's—one of learning, encouragement and listening to the still, small, zephyr-like voice of God amid the roaring clamour of everyday life. Journeying through this book with you has taught me so much, not only about writing a book but also about the God I follow and the daughter he has made me to be. There's one thing that has become particularly apparent to me, one thing that I need to continually remind myself of: *I will never be enough.*

However much I try to get the grades that will please my teachers, and however much I strive to win my friends' acceptance or my family's approval, I will never be good enough. The goalposts in these situations always change. As soon as I tick one box, more requirements are added (often by me), pushing me to do and be more to attain that elusive standard of perfection.

The standard God sets for holy, righteous living is different; it doesn't shift or change. Instead, it remains impossibly high—literally impossibly. I can never hope to achieve God's approval by living perfectly in my own strength. I am weak and powerless to do it: I will always fall short because of my sin.

Despite the seeming negativity of this message, I would suggest that it is a message of great hope. It is hopeful because it shows us that the only way to live is on our knees, asking humbly for help so that we are reconciled to God. This humble posture is possible only when we realise that, by ourselves, we can never be good enough for God.

But where does help come from? It comes from the Lord, the Maker of heaven and earth (check out Psalm 121). In my prayer journal, I once wrote this: 'The gospel is this: you will never be enough, but "He has done it!" (Psalm 22:31) for you. Because of God's great love, Christ died for the not-enoughs, to bring them to God.' It's so true: our help comes from God, who loves us back to life. But *how*? I think we have answered this question throughout the previous chapters, but let me tell you one last story, from John 4.

She leans the broom up against the wall and unhooks the bucket from beside the door. 'Noon-time is hot and tiring,' she thinks, 'but I really have to have that water.' So she sets out, her skin burning slightly in the outdoor heat.

Dust clings to her skirt as she walks towards Jacob's Well. She feels world-worn and weary, the confusing worries of life having sapped the vibrancy of her soul until it's become easier to ignore her heart and live every day the same.

Yet today isn't the same, she realises, as she spots a man in the distance, a stranger, sitting next to the well.

Fear lurches inside her, a needling sensation that makes her set her face into a mask of indifference so that she will betray no vulnerable feeling. 'Why must there be someone there?' she thinks. 'At least he looks well-travelled. He won't know my story—my past, my mistakes... my pain. At least I'll be able to hide that from him.'

The woman reaches the well. Studiously ignoring the man (yet curiously hoping that he will notice her), she lowers the bucket into the cool earth, the rope passing through her hands until the bucket hits the pool at the bottom.

'Will you give me a drink?'

The woman looks up, startled. He spoke to her! His voice sounded full of empathy, as if he had seen many things and understood. Kind eyes look up at her… but… is he…? Yes, he is. Jewish. How disappointing.

Straightening up from her bent posture, the woman gazes unflinchingly into the stranger's face: 'You are a Jew and I am a Samaritan woman. How can you ask me for a drink?' It's unheard of, and it's confusing. Surely he knows where he is… right in the middle of a Samaritan village? When he realises his mistake, he won't be so kind. But would he listen to her even if he wasn't a Jew?

He gazes back, equally unflinchingly, unnerving her slightly. As well as kindness, there is fire in his eyes—something powerful, compelling. His words are even more surprising: 'If you knew the gift of God and who it is that asks you for a drink, you would have asked him and he would have given you living water.'

The woman's weary heart awakes and stirs at the words 'living water', as if they are an answer to something, as if this man knows what she longs for most. Despite these deep feelings, all she can say is, 'Sir, you have nothing to draw with and the well is deep. Where can you get this living water?'

The fire still blazes in the man's eyes as he replies, 'Everyone who drinks this water will be thirsty again, but whoever drinks the water I give them will never thirst. Indeed, the water I give them will become in them a spring of water welling up to eternal life.'

The woman's heart races, and now a keen hunger stirs within her. The bucket lies forgotten at the bottom of the well as she exclaims, 'Sir, give me this water!'

He replies, 'Go, call your husband and come back.'

'I have no husband.' Does this mean she won't be allowed living water? She turns back to the well, hiding her pain and disappointment as she draws up the bucket, offering it to the man with an indifferent expression. She represses the hunger in her eyes.

After he has drunk from his cupped hands, the man reclines and begins to tell her about her husbands, her history, her story. Although he has never seen her before, he knows. He knows everything: it's as if he has seen past her defences and straight into her heart.

Recovering from her shock, the woman says, 'I can see that you are a prophet. Our ancestors worshipped on this mountain, but you Jews claim that the place where we must worship is in Jerusalem.'

'Believe me, a time is coming when you will worship the Father neither on this mountain nor in Jerusalem. True worshippers worship the Father in spirit and in truth, for they are the kind of worshippers the Father seeks.' The man speaks with confidence, but how can he? How can he authoritatively speak of what God desires?

'I know that Messiah is coming. When he comes, he will explain everything to us.' Despite her trials and pain, the woman's fragile hope is still intact. She still hopes that one day everything will change and she will be free. She just doesn't expect that day to come any time soon.

The man sits up straight, looks her in the eye and says, 'I, the one speaking to you—I am he. I am the Messiah.'

Jesus offered living water to a woman who was hurt, expecting nothing and feeling trapped and lonely. Imagine how she felt when Jesus revealed his identity to her. It's no wonder that she ran back to her town and told everyone of the Messiah-man she had met at Jacob's Well. Many believed her, too, as her testimony was backed up by a transformation in her soul. They no longer saw a scared, defensive, lonely woman, but a joyful, beautiful woman, radiant with God's grace. Jesus had released the woman's caged heart, letting her live free.

Jesus extends grace after grace after grace to those who are willing to open up their hearts to him. He pours love and forgiveness on to his children and strengthens them to live fully and joyfully. He offers *you* a cup of living, everlasting water.

Max Lucado writes, 'Don't you need regular sips from God's reservoir? I do. I've offered this prayer in countless situations... Many times a day I step to the underground spring of God and receive anew his work for my sin and death, the energy of his Spirit, his Lordship and his love.'[35] Jesus offers thirst-quenching, life-giving grace-water from the reservoir of his heart. He has already completed your salvation and has forgiven you your sin and your inability to be 'enough'. He's giving you life and freedom in a cup of water, a gift for you to take and taste.

As we draw to the end of this book, we can see that striving to be good, smart, pretty or holy enough is not what we're made for. What makes us who we are meant to be is the realisation that, on our own, we will never be enough. We need grace-water to well up inside us, giving us strength and sustenance straight from God's hand.

I stumbled across these words, in Shauna Niequist's blog:

You're enough because you were created by God, out of nothing but dust and love, and that's what makes you enough. You're not enough because you're smart enough or pretty enough or working hard enough—although you are, to be sure, all those things: brilliant and beautiful and working your tail off. But that's not what makes you enough.

What makes you enough is your createdness. God made you. He made you, dreamed you up, spun you out of thin air. That makes you so much more than enough. That makes you a work of art—because you were created by a master.[36]

Lovely girl, *you are enough*. You are enough because God breathed life into your body. He gave your heart a rhythm and a purpose. You are enough because there is a beautiful, God-given spark of creativity and personality right at the core of who you are, beauty humming at your centre. You are enough and will always be enough because of God's grace, his unending love for you.

Hold these truths as you close this book. Don't let the words that God has written on your heart fade and fall into forgetfulness. Instead, live them. Let this book be a step taken towards a life lived to the full, as Jesus promised (John 10:10). Live life beautiful, big, vibrant, seeking God's love and grace in every situation, knowing that you are enough in him.

Resources

At the end of John's Gospel, we read, 'There are so many other things Jesus did. If they were all written down, each of them, one by one, I can't imagine a world big enough to hold such a library of books' (21:25, THE MESSAGE).

In my tattered red Bible, I have written underneath the words, 'So human'. I think what I meant was that John, in writing these words, shows such an unexpected, refreshing and relatable amazement at the powerful things that Jesus did. And what he says is true, I think. If everyone did write a book containing their thoughts on what Jesus has done in this world, there would be no library big enough to hold all the paper, ink, words and stories.

However, we sure are trying! There are so many books, blogs and songs dedicated to sharing Jesus' life and love with the world. There are so many millions of words for you to be strengthened and encouraged by as you learn the rhythm of God's heart. Below, I've compiled a small library of really good things to read or listen to. Their authors have such a heart and passion for God. Perhaps you could add your own suggestions to social media with the hashtag #createdenough.

Finally, although all these resources are fantastically helpful, they are incomparable to God's word, the Bible. Think of the Bible as daily bread, and these books, blogs and songs as cake. They taste good and encourage and energise you, but ultimately it's the bread that will sustain you. Read and listen to these words, but always remember who they're pointing to—our loving, sovereign, Saviour God. In the words of Charles Spurgeon: 'Visit many good books but live in the Bible.'[37]

Books

- Jennifer Dukes Lee, *Love Idol* (Tyndale Momentum, 2014)
- Philip Yancey, *What's So Amazing About Grace?* (Zondervan, 2002)
- Jefferson Bethke, *Jesus > Religion: Why he is so much better than trying harder, doing more and being good enough* (Thomas Nelson, 2013)
- Emily P. Freeman, *A Million Little Ways* (Revell, 2013)
- C.S. Lewis, *Mere Christianity* (Collins, 2012)
- Tim Hawkins, *Totally Transformed* (The Good Book Company, 2010)
- Ann Voskamp, *One Thousand Gifts* (Zondervan, 2010)
- Pete Greig, *Red Moon Rising* (David C. Cook, 2004)
- Krish Kandiah, *Dysciples* (Authentic, 2009)
- Max Lucado, *Come Thirsty* (W Publishing, 2010)
- Jo Swinney, *God Hunting* (Scripture Union, 2011)

For Bible study:

- Vaughan Roberts, *God's Big Picture* (IVP, 2009)
- *Engage* Bible notes, produced every three months by The Good Book Company. These are daily Bible studies that take you through a Bible passage with insightful questions and opportunities for prayer.
- Gordon D. Fee, *How to Read the Bible For All Its Worth* (Zondervan, 2003)

Blogs and websites

Each blog listed below speaks words of hope, love and peace into the everyday struggles of life and encourages us to live a life of fullness and risk with God. They're grace-filled spaces focusing on God, connecting you with him and others who may be experiencing similar situations. As creators and keepers of these sites, the authors have kindly invited you to visit their corners of the internet and see something of God reflected in their words.

- More Precious (http://moreprecious.co.uk): 'More Precious is a blog with a vision for encouraging girls to be strong and distinctive in their Christian faith. We publish miniblogs, devotionals, interviews, testimonies and regular posts from our core team, in the hope that you might be encouraged by God's faithfulness and love, and inspired to keep pursuing Jesus in every sphere of your life. Do feel free to contact More Precious at lucy@moreprecious.co.uk for more information about the blog, events or if you have any questions.' (Lucy Beauchamp, co-founder of and author at More Precious)
- Rhythms (rhythms.org): 'The Rhythms community is a growing movement who are living differently. Although issues like poverty, climate change and inequality seem like insurmountable challenges, we believe that by taking small, everyday actions we can create a change in us and in the world around us. When these actions are done regularly, habits of lasting change develop. We call these rhythms, and we'd love for you to join us on this journey. Start being the change today by signing up at rhythms. org or downloading the app.' (Katherine Maxwell-Cook, editor of Tearfund's Rhythms)

- Chatting At The Sky (http://emilypfreeman.com): 'Chatting At The Sky is a space I've been writing for nine years, sharing my own photos and personal stories. I hope you see something hopeful here, something that calls courage out from places within you that maybe you forgot were there, something that resonates with you as a person. I'm deeply curious about the mystery of Christ, the gracefulness of the everyday, and the sacredness of our inner lives. Everything I write or speak about comes from this curiosity and the deep conviction that every need, desire, and expectation is met in the person of Jesus Christ. As you visit Chatting At the Sky may you always find a place where your soul can breathe.' (Emily Freeman, author of Chatting At The Sky and several books including *A Million Little Ways*)

- *threads* (www.threadsuk.com): '*threads* are a collective of Christians from all walks of life, who are living, working and trying to carve out our identity in our worlds. We are artists and bankers. We are singles and we're marrieds. We are visionaries and geeks, hilarious and deadly serious. We are scratching our heads about faith and life and what they have to say about each other. We are curious. We are wrestling with questions where there used to be answers, and are passionate about working it out together. We are celebrating each other's talents. We're inspired, and we're hopeful. We are *threads*. Join the conversation at threadsUK.com.' (Thomas McConaghie, *threads* writer and coordinator)

- The Sophia Network (http://blog.sophianetwork.org.uk): 'The Sophia Network exists to empower and equip women in leadership, and to champion the full equality of women and men in the church. We believe that God created men and women to work together in partnership and full equality, and that both women and men are called to leadership in all areas of life. We have a particular focus on connecting women in leadership to access training, develop skills and grow as leaders. We also want to encourage both men and women to reflect on the role models they provide for young people, and the aspirations and expectations they are helping to shape. Come and visit us at www.sophianetwork.org.uk to read more of the work we do, and be encouraged, inspired and challenged in your walk with God.' (Sharon Prior, co-founder of the Sophia Network)

- A Girl Like Me (agirlikeme.com): 'Being a girl is tough. With so many different messages pouring in, it can be hard to determine what is truth and what is a lie. Sometimes we get it right, and sometimes we fail miserably. We know, we've been there. A Girl Like Me hopes to come alongside you to help weed out the lies and come to a place of truth and healing. We don't want to sugarcoat or hide behind our failures, but instead embrace the grace that Jesus freely gives us. For you, the lonely, the broken, the scared and the unwanted—take heart. You aren't the only one feeling messed up in this crazy world. You're just another girl... like me. Come and meet us at agirlikeme.com, a place made for you to find encouragement, grace and truth.' (Heather, founder and writer at A Girl Like Me)

- A Holy Experience (aholyexperience.com): This is the blog of Ann Voskamp. She is a truly amazing author and I've quoted her many times throughout this book. Read more of her beautiful words at aholyexperience.com and be challenged, inspired and refreshed.

- 24–7 Prayer (www.24-7prayer.com): This is where you can find all the information you need about the 24–7 prayer movement, including podcasts, poems, manuals for setting up prayer rooms, blog posts, and news. It's inspirational.

- Acorn Christian Healing Foundation (www.acornchristian. org): Acorn works to equip people with listening and reconciliation skills, bringing healing and wholeness to individuals, churches and communities. This website contains information about their work and vision. Take a look: it could be something that would be good for your church or youth group to be involved with.

Music

Below are some bands and artists and some of their tracks and albums that you may enjoy listening to.

- Tenth Avenue North (albums: *Over and Underneath*; *The Struggle*; *Cathedrals*; *The Light Meets the Dark*)
- David Crowder Band (tracks: 'How he loves'; 'Sometimes'; 'Holy')
- Gungor (tracks: 'Beautiful things'; 'We will run')
- Aaron Keyes (tracks: 'Dwell'; 'Sovereign over us')
- Rend Collective (albums: *Campfire*; *The Art of Celebration*)
- MercyMe (track: 'Greater')
- Matt Redman: (album: *Ten Thousand Reasons*)
- Owl City (tracks: 'Embers'; 'Shooting star'; 'You're not alone'; 'In Christ alone')

Notes

1 Augustine of Hippo, *Confessions*, quoted at www.goodreads.com/quotes/42572-thou-hast-made-us-for-thyself-o-lord-and-our

2 Ann Voskamp, 'How to stay sane in a spinning world' (25 September 2014): www.aholyexperience.com/2014/09/how-to-stay-sane-in-a-spinning-world/

3 Jefferson Bethke, *Jesus > Religion: Why he is so much better than trying harder, doing more and being good enough* (Thomas Nelson, 2013), p. 140

4 Theodore Roosevelt, quoted at www.aholyexperience.com/2015/04/when-you-feel-you-are-not-enough

5 Heather Owen, 'Keeping up appearances' (17 September 2014): http://agirlikeme.com/keeping-up-appearances

6 Pete Greig, 'The vision': www.24-7prayer.com/thevisionpoem

7 William Shakespeare, *King Lear*, Act I Scene 4

8 Philip Yancey, *What's So Amazing About Grace?* (Zondervan, 2002), p. 69

9 Emily P. Freeman, *A Million Little Ways* (Revell, 2013), p. 175

10 Definition found at http://dictionary.reference.com/browse/shalom

11 Ann Voskamp, *One Thousand Gifts* (Zondervan, 2010), pp. 170–171

12 Ray Markham, *Bit Part Prophets of the Bible* (CWR, date), p. 56

13 Ann Voskamp's words on this are beautiful: read them in full at 'The secret you have to know about you & that thing you're going through' (25 March 2014): www.aholyexperience.com/2014/03/letters-to-daughters-the-secret-you-have-to-know-about-you-that-thing-youre-going-through

14 Jennifer Dukes Lee, *Love Idol* (Tyndale Momentum, 2014), p. 235

15 Yancey, *What's So Amazing About Grace?*, p. 54

16 Bethke, *Jesus > Religion*, p. 28

17 Libby Vincent, 'The BIG difference between guilt and shame' (29 January 2015): www.theveryworstmissionary. com/2015/01/guilt-vs-shame-part-2-theres-big.html

18 Dr Kelly Flanagan, 'The best way to guarantee a blog post will not be shared on Facebook' (20 February 2013), http:// drkellyflanagan.com/2013/02/20/the-best-way-to-guarantee- a-blog-post-will-not-be-shared-on-facebook

19 Bethke, *Jesus > Religion*, p. 77

20 Bethke, *Jesus > Religion*, p. 8

21 www.ok.co.uk

22 www.hellomagazine.com

23 www.closeronline.co.uk

24 Krish Kandiah, *Dysciples* (Authentic, 2009), p. 7

25 Kelsey Kirkegaard, 'Out with the safe' (18 February 2015): http://agirlikeme.com/out-with-the-safe

26 C.S. Lewis, *Mere Christianity* (HarperCollins, 2012), p. 34

27 C.J. Mahaney, *Living the Cross-Centred Life* (Multnomah, 2006), p. 35

28 See www.prayercourse.org

29 Ann Voskamp, Tweet (20 February 2015): https://twitter.com/ annvoskamp/status/568740937582706688

30 Emily Freeman, 'How your morning pages may become a sacred space' (5 October 2013): http://emilypfreeman.com/ morning-pages

31 L.M. Montgomery, *Anne of Green Gables* (Puffin, 1977), p. 47

32 Emily Freeman, 'Becoming a soul minimalist' (16 February 2015): http://emilypfreeman.com/becoming-soul-minimalist/

33 Mahaney, *Living the Cross-Centred Life*, p. 34

34 Jo Swinney, *God Hunting* (Scripture Union, 2011), p. 21

35 Max Lucado, *Come Thirsty* (W Publishing, 2010), p. 16

36 Shauna Neiquist, 'You are enough' (26 February 2015): www. shaunaniequist.com/you-are-enough

37 Charles Haddon Spurgeon, quoted at www.goodreads.com/ quotes/391924-visit-many-good-books-but-live-in-the-bible

Postcards from Heaven

Words and pictures to help you hear from God

Ellie Hart

'My heart's desire is that this book could become a place where you can encounter our wonderful, beautiful, untameable, passionate, loving God and hear him speak directly to you, whatever your circumstances.'

Writer and artist Ellie Hart has created a series of 'postcards from heaven'— her own paintings linked to short, thought-provoking reflections, to help all who long to hear more clearly from God, especially when going through seasons of change and uncertainty.

ISBN 978 0 85746 427 9   £7.99
Available from your local Christian bookshop or direct from BRF: please visit www.brfonline.org.uk

Enjoyed
this book?

Write a review—we'd love to hear what you think.
Email: reviews@brf.org.uk

Keep up to date—receive details of our new books as they happen.
Sign up for email news and select your interest groups at:
www.brfonline.org.uk/findoutmore/

Follow us on Twitter @brfonline

By post—to receive new title information by post (UK only), complete the form below and post to: BRF Mailing Lists, 15 The Chambers, Vineyard, Abingdon, Oxfordshire, OX14 3FE

Your Details
Name _____
Address_____
_____
Town/City _____ Post Code _____
Email _____

Your Interest Groups (*Please tick as appropriate)

❏ Advent/Lent	❏ Messy Church
❏ Bible Reading & Study	❏ Pastoral
❏ Children's Books	❏ Prayer & Spirituality
❏ Discipleship	❏ Resources for Children's Church
❏ Leadership	❏ Resources for Schools

Support your local bookshop
Ask about their new title information schemes.